Contents

Multicultural Connections

Creative Writing, Literature, and Assessment in the Elementary School

Norma Sadler

scarecrow education

The Scarecrow Press, Inc.
A Scarecrow Education Book
Lanham, Maryland, and London
2002

SCARECROW PRESS, INC.
A Scarecrow Education Book

Published in the United States of America
by Scarecrow Press, Inc.
4720 Boston Way, Lanham, Maryland 20706
www.scaroweducation.com

4 Pleydell Gardens, Folkestone
Kent CT20 2DN, England

British Library Cataloguing in Publication Information Available

Library of Congress Cataloging-in-Publication Data

Sadler, Norma.
    Multicultural connections : creative writing, literature, and assessment in
the elementary school / Norma Sadler.
        p. cm.—(A Scarecrow education book)
    Includes bibliographical references and index.
    ISBN 0-8108-4180-0 (pbk. : alk. paper)
    1. English language—Composition and exercises—Study and teaching
(Elementary) 2. Creative writing—Study and teaching (Elementary)
3. Multicultural education. 4. Children's literature—Study and teaching
(Elementary) I. Title. II. Series.
LB1576 .S23 2002
372.6'044—dc21   Library of Congress Control Number: 2001049085

♾️™ The paper used in this publication meets the minimum requirements
of American National Standard for Information Sciences—Permanence of
Paper for Printed Library Materials, ANSI/NISO Z39.48-1992.
Manufactured in the United States of America.

I Watched an Eagle Soar

Grandmother,
I watched an eagle soar
high in the sky
until a cloud covered him up.
Grandmother,
I still saw the eagle
behind my eyes

> from *Dancing Teepees: Poems of American Indian Youth*,
> by Virginia Driving Hawk Sneve.

This striking image of an eagle in "I Watched an Eagle Soar" shows the writer's power of observation. First, the character in the poem, the *persona* adopted by the author, sees an eagle and later sees it even after the eagle has disappeared in a cloud. The whole image is a fine metaphor for how a writer thinks while creating a poem, a short story, or a novel from past observations. A writer takes images, connects them to other images or ideas, and turns them into a piece of creative writing. It sounds simple, but of course it isn't.

Young writers, trying to write stories of their own, need to understand what children's book authors do when they write. They need to know how these authors write. And it does help for young writers, as it would help all of us who write, to know where authors get their ideas for what they create in fiction.

But how do you, as teachers, get students to understand what writers do when they write fiction? To help your students not only understand what writers do but also be able to apply that knowledge about the craft of writing fiction to their own writing, you need the answers to some specific questions:

- What do writers take from what they see or know from their own experience to come up with the stories that they write?
- How do the stories that authors write reflect who they are and what is important to them?
- Why do the stories "work" so that readers are willing to become engaged and go with them wherever authors wish to take them? Basically, why do readers read what authors write for them?

In this book, writers speak about their writing from multicultural perspectives. Sections on the elements of fiction writing show young writers what they need to know to become more skilled in the "craft" of writing fiction.

A JOURNEY THROUGH THE FICTION WRITING PROCESS

This book is a journey in the process of fiction writing. Along the way, you will learn about literary elements and become familiar with ways to use multicultural children's literature to teach fiction writing. You will hear what authors of children's books say about various parts of the writing process. Finally, you will be able to engage young writers in a variety of activities to strengthen their own fiction writing.

CONNECTIONS TO WRITING IN THE CLASSROOM

Students need to be able to write and write well. For that to happen, they need an understanding of the writing process and they need to engage in writing activities. To further those goals, teachers have created reading and writing workshops and have used children's literature and its authors as sources and models for student writing. Also in those workshops, teachers have asked students to create narratives that include literary elements such as character, setting, plot, point of view, theme, and tone. They have even assessed student writing for these elements and the development of an "authorial voice," which is a part of style.

Chapter 9, "Assessment: Do Young Writers Know How to Write Fiction?," offers structured ways to approach critiques of student writing. That chapter is worth previewing before you use the strategies in this book. Also, the bibliography gives you sources for writers workshop goals, formats, and materials.

CONNECTIONS TO READING
MULTICULTURAL CHILDREN'S LITERATURE

In the last ten years, more diverse perspectives in literature have been included in literature-based textbooks and trade books, specifically in genres such as picture storybooks, chapter books, and novels.

Additional author studies, such as Carol Brennan Jenkins's *The Allure of Authors*, verify the importance of students studying authors and the literature that they write so that students understand the children's literature written for them.

With the greater availability of multicultural literature in all genres of children's literature and author perspectives on that literature available, you should find it easier to include more diverse children's literature in your classroom reading activities. With your increased use of multicultural children's literature in reading activities, you will be able to use that same literature in more writing activities.

FINDING A VOICE IN WRITING

When you merge reading and writing in writers workshops, you encourage the development of the diverse writing voices of your students. You can teach students how to write in diverse voices that reflect their own cultures or backgrounds. By working with literary elements from fictional genres, such as contemporary realistic fiction, fantasy, folktales, and historical fiction, young writers can connect the craft of fiction writing with their own voices to convey "story."

It makes sense that if children read about characters who are the same gender or ethnic background as themselves, they can more easily identify with a story and see themselves vicariously participate in the story. When young writers extend from that reading and "write" themselves or their own backgrounds into story, they strengthen their own manner of writing. They can make this connection happen by developing the specific skills of fiction writing.

WHO WE ARE SHAPES OUR VIEW
OF THE WORLD AND OUR WRITING

What we go through as children becomes a part of us, helps to define us, and helps to make us who we are as adults. Both Shonto Begay, Navaho author and illustrator, and Uri Orlev, Israeli author, show us how, as children, they understood the world around them and how that world influenced their adult world. Shonto Begay:

> It was in my youth that I learned to see the world around me. I learned to savor the beauty and to feel at home among the red mesas, piñon, and juniper. My world was the circular line of the horizon. . . . I have always had a love for art. To re-create facets of my universe in its varying images was the adventure of living. Through my eyes and hands, I drew my first line upon a slick rock.[1]

As a Jew in occupied Poland during World War II, Uri Orlev survived the Holocaust. He carried his observations and perceptions of childhood into adulthood. He speaks about how important his experiences as a young Jewish child in a Polish ghetto are to his writing:

> A woman once called to speak to me about one of the books I had written on this subject. At one point she asked, "Did writing this book enable you to 'finish' with the Holocaust?" I replied that I cannot "finish" with it because I went through it as a child. It is perhaps possible that adults, adult writers, are able to "finish" with the Holocaust, though I find it difficult to believe. I certainly cannot because I don't wish to, because what other people call the Holocaust was, for me, my childhood.[2]

Uri Orlev's novel *The Island on Bird Street* tells the story about a Jewish child, a fictional character who survives the Holocaust. Uri Orlev convinces readers to go with him to a historic time and place. Young readers, as "critics," can see how Uri Orlev crafts his stories by studying specific literary elements, such as characters, setting, plot, or point of view, in his books. Finally, these young readers/critics can become young writers and "model" from Uri Orlev and others to create new stories.

CONNECTIONS WITH MULTICULTURAL CHILDREN'S LITERATURE

When you read a book of multicultural literature aloud or your students read it on their own, you might choose to include reader response activities that involve speaking, listening, reading, or writing skills. You might ask for personal responses from students, such as their thoughts, feelings, or experiences in relation to the book read aloud or read on their own. Personal responses connect literature to the lives of children. To connect to the lives of the diverse students in your classroom and offer global connections to all students, you need to provide access to multicultural literature that reflects diverse cultures—literature that "speaks" to students in particular ways and gives them a chance to gain insight into their own lives. For example, children's literature that makes use of different dialects or languages other than English adds a dimension of another culture to the story. Diverse students see their own cultures valued and see their own cultural perspectives reinforced. That connection can enhance what Patricia Enciso calls their "cultural imaginations" and "inform their sense of identity."[3]

Of course, students of all cultural backgrounds benefit from a wide selection of multicultural stories in the classroom. And when students begin to write their own stories, they will have a diverse reading background from which to build and model their own writing. By modeling from the best writers and illustrators of various diverse pieces of literature, young writers can express cultural aspects of their own identities. They can create stories that are not only authentic to who they are and their particular cultures, but also authentic in a universal sense, to connect each of us to one another. Joseph Bruchac makes that point clearly:

> One of the reasons I have devoted so much of my own life to the understanding and the respectful telling of traditional Native stories is my

strong belief that now, more than ever, these tales have much to teach us—whether we are of Native ancestry or not. We learn about ourselves by understanding others.[4]

To give the students the chance to create stories that offer them the same possibility that Joseph Bruchac has is to give them the chance to merge their lives and experiences with their imaginations to create their own stories.

All students should encounter a variety of multicultural literature in classrooms. In order for that to happen, González-Jensen and Sadler believe that teachers should "take the initiative to be as inclusive as possible across a variety of cultures in the books chosen for classroom use."[5]

By sharing diverse perspectives through written activities, students communicate their own backgrounds, either in writing about literature they have read or in their own creative writing. In this book, young writers can learn with your help about how authors have connected to their childhoods to be able to write their books. Margarita González-Jensen, a bilingual author of children's literature, shares her childhood memories connected to multicultural literature:

> Question: "Can you remember connecting your own background to the world of the school?"
>
> Margarita González-Jensen: "I never saw my world connected. That's why I am writing now."[6]

For students now, there is a rich array of literature in classrooms for them to model from for fiction writing. Authors do write from what they know and imagine, and children, like them, should have the opportunity to do so as well.

Strategies in this text will assist you with integrating the culture/diversity of the students with whom you work in the classroom with multicultural literature. At the same time, students will be developing their own skills in creative writing.

STORYTELLING AND STORY "WRITING"

If children are acquainted with "the way stories work" and storytelling at an early age, they develop a sense of story structure. Students have heard storytelling in their lives in school or away from school. How many of us have heard about writers/storytellers who say that they heard stories from their mothers, fathers, or grandparents? These relatives remembered the stories and created new stories to tell about their lives. What rich possibilities arise from those stories for student writing!

Alma Flor Ada speaks about the connections of lives and dreams with the importance of reading and writing as well as the amount of time she spends in revision and rewriting:

Question: "What advice do you have for young writers?"

Alma Flor Ada: "I personally believe that we learn to write by reading. So my first advice is to read, read, read. The next is to approach the writing as you would a joyful experience, with anticipation of what you will discover inside your mind which you did not even suspect was awaiting there to be awakened. Write for yourself, for enjoyment, to create a character that will become a new friend in your life, to tell a story that you feel entertaining, to share the treasure of your own feelings, to honor the people in your life by telling their history. . . . Once you have begun writing, know that you can keep what you wrote and rewrite and polish it as much as you want. Sometimes I work on the same story for months. I have a book that I worked on for twenty years. When I finally felt it was ready, I sent it to a contest and it won a big award. This book *Encaje de piedra* (which won the Marta Salotti gold medal in Argentina) continues to give me joy, because I never abandoned it and got to finish it. Never be afraid to write as you speak, as you feel, as you dream, as you think. And value your words—they can be great gifts to others and to yourself."[7]

Students' personal narratives can be used to develop aspects of writing such as tone and voice. By elaborating and extending their own personal narratives, young writers can move those narratives closer to fictional narratives. In the process, they will understand how story structure works for their own personal narratives and learn how to use that story structure in the construction of their own fiction.

Question: "How could teachers encourage children to write about their own background and not leave it at the schoolhouse door?"

Margarita González-Jensen: "Home stories are a good way to encourage children to write. They get kids to feel at ease with their writing—they can take elements of what they heard about relatives or tell about something that happened. In the past, children were given a blank sheet of paper and told to 'write.' Children need a teacher to tell them that there are valuable experiences already in their heads—that they have things to write about that will give them confidence as writers."[8]

The writing of fiction demands that writers understand story or narrative in both oral and written form. Again, if students can understand story early on, then they will be able to write stories of their own.

Question: "Are there any events/stories from your childhood that have turned into a plot or event in one of your books?"

Eric Kimmel: "It isn't so much the events as the stories themselves. I first heard stories about Hershel Ostropolier [*Hershel and the Hanukkah Goblins, The Adventures of Hershel of Ostropol*] and the people of Chelm [*The Jar of Fools*] when I was a little boy. I had a terrific religious education at the East Midwood Jewish Center. That's where I began my love of Bible stories [*Be Not Far from Me*]. One of my favorite books was my collection of Grimm's Fairy Tales with the Fritz Kredl illustrations. Many of my books are retellings from Grimm. Also, my grandma, who was an extremely powerful influence, told me lots of stories about her childhood in Ukraine, as well as lots of Ukrainian peasant and animal stories. That's why I love Ukrainian and Russian tales [*The Bird's Gift*; *One Eye, Two Eyes, and Three Eyes*; *Sirko and the Wolf*]. In one sense, most of my career is built on sharing stories I loved as a child with children today."[9]

In addition, when students have a chance to hear, to tell, and to write stories, they are creating text structures in their own minds, extending their backgrounds and expanding their own thinking and imagination about their lives and experiences. When story structures and the structures of literary elements are within their grasp to add to their own writing experiences, young writers can concentrate on the development of their fictional writing because they will have the tools of the trade to go further in their writing.

Learning how to work with elements in defined ways frees young writers to be the "authors of their work." They are also free to work with their own personal experiences or imaginary ones, having already solved problems connected with understanding and applying literary elements and story structure to their writing. Understanding story and working with literary elements frees young writers to write.

This book, with its focus on literary elements and the application of those elements, gives students a chance to learn to use narrative in their writing. For some students, that may mean that they will be able to craft not just short stories but also chapter books or novels.

Enhancing student writing development and assessing that development allows you as teachers to help diverse students to have authentic voices in their writing.

THE IMPORTANCE OF MODELING ON OTHERS

Present authors of multicultural children's literature had role models—writers—who influenced them as readers in their childhood or adulthood.

Question: "What Mexican children's authors influenced you as a reader?"

Margarita González-Jensen: "There were none when I was young out there. As an adult, Alma Flor Ada. In college, I was exposed to Mexican and Spanish writers. I knew the poem *Margarita* by Ruben Dario, because my grandmother had read it to my mother as a little girl, and she memorized stanzas and recited it to me. There was music in my life as a child—songs and records—Cricri—well known in Mexico for children's songs."[10]

The authors and the children's literature in this book are diverse models for students to value and understand that their own cultural backgrounds have worth in their writing. Because I have focused on fiction writing in this book, I have chosen authors who are fiction writers. Their stories convey cultural connections to their backgrounds. For example, Alma Flor Ada heard North American folk tales and *The Tale of Peter Rabbit* by Beatrix Potter as a child. She connects those tales together in *Dear Peter Rabbit* and *Yours Truly, Goldilocks*.

Like Alma Flor Ada, other writers take on or internalize the cultural connections of their own or the dominant culture of the country that they are in, from schooling perhaps. But also, and more importantly, they keep the cultural and social connections of where they grew up. Katherine Paterson, an internationally recognized author, has a background of growing up in China and the United States, and as an adult, living in Japan as well as in the United States. Because of her keen observation, ability to research, and her writing talent that communicates cultural background in story form, she is able to give us culturally authentic fictional multicultural books that take place in Japan, China, and the United States. Her characters, settings, and plots are not only excellent children's literature, but also clearer pictures of cultures to which she has connected, holding them dear for all of us.

HOW WRITERS ENGAGE IN THE COMPOSING PROCESS

Each of us who writes approaches the writing process differently. For example, I sit down and write notes about what I want to write. I may even sketch out some scenes with a few words, then I go back and develop those scenes into pages of writing. I may take several breaks, especially if what I am working on requires much concentration. I may write long notes that wind around the page when I wish to make a change. I may doodle, draw a picture or time line. But then there was the time that flying back from Mexico, I wrote three scenes in three short sentences on a napkin that turned into a 4,000-word short story.

In a speech at a conference years ago, Eric Kimmel talked about walking his dog, checking the mail, going to the library, and then all of a sudden in a burst of energy sitting down to write for a time frame that was forty-five minutes. But what went into his time frame, I am sure, was research, thinking, and sorting, until the words came to rest on a page.

As a teacher, you have to consider whether or not all of your students will be able to write in certain preset classroom conditions and whether there are alternatives for those students. While some students will find a classroom atmosphere quite appropriate for composing, others will not. Some may need to work in a quiet area—"a studio," a place where they can really think and write. Some can work anywhere. Each of us has our own inner "atmosphere," for the way we observe, perceive, and write, that is connected to how we learn and express ourselves.

To assist writers in the process of writing, this book gives material in different ways to students—from linear and written formats to spatial ones, such as charts and graphs. Different subject areas such as art and music are included as ways to work with student writing.

If you work with students on writing, you will furnish them with the tools of the trade to extend narrative from descriptions or paragraphs to short stories, chapter books, novels, or perhaps the experimental fiction of the future that we can only imagine. For a classroom community of diverse learners, this book is dynamic, allowing for a variety of possible uses to meet your needs in working with young writers on fiction writing.

ORGANIZATION OF THE BOOK

This book lays out specific strategies for fiction writing and assessment of that writing in grades K–6. Since there are many activities for each section on literary elements, the book values your class—the community of diverse learners—and gives you an opportunity to pick and choose which skills your students need help with most in fiction writing. As students work from and model on some of the best authors of multicultural literature, perhaps they may see themselves as writers who are able not only to express themselves well in fictional writing, but in other forms of writing as well.

Literary Elements

Most of the chapters have a literary element as a focus, with authors and books to go with that element. Block quotes give information in an author's own words on everything from ideas and childhood to literary elements and books. These sections will provide you with a better understanding of how authors reflect their own cultures—their voices speaking directly to you, the reader, and, by extension, to your students as future writers. Sharing these "voices" with students, especially the voices of authors who give advice to young writers, will give insights into multicultural perspectives as well as insights into the writing process itself.

Journal Activities

Each chapter on a literary element has one or more journal activities. Having a place to keep drawings, notes, or ideas for stories is an important habit for young writers to develop.

Virginia Driving Hawk Sneve, Lakota Sioux, discusses the importance of keeping a journal:

> Question: "What advice do you have for young writers?"
>
> Virginia Driving Hawk Sneve: "Read. Read. Reading exposes you to the way words are used in good stories. It builds your vocabulary so that your writing can build images in readers' minds the way great authors have done. Reading is also the way a writer finds out what has been written and what needs to be written. I also encourage children to write every day. Keep a journal and write about what you've done, seen, heard, smelled, and how you felt. Then in school, learn to use the tools of writing—the grammar, the spelling, etc. And finally, keep at it. Don't be discouraged by not being published on your first try. My first book wasn't published until I was thirty-five, after long years of trying."[11]

Likewise, Paul Goble keeps notes and ideas, but not in a journal format:

> I do not keep a journal but when I am working on a book I have a file in which I keep sheets of notes. Whenever I have an idea which I think might be useful, I put it in the file before I forget it. Most of such notes I never use, but some prove useful.[12]

Strategies for Identification/Assessment of Literary Elements

Each chapter includes strategies for building and assessing knowledge and practice.

The activities are set up so that you may pick and choose to develop specific skills as appropriate. While many of the activities could be used as assessments for various elements, at least one of them in each chapter is designated as an oral or a written assessment for the literary element in that chapter. For overall assessment, chapter 9 focuses on ways to tie fiction writing to possible overall curriculum goals on writing.

Appendixes

Because there are a variety of multicultural books for you included in this book, you should be able to locate some of the books from the authors listed in Appendix 1: Selected Bibliography of Authors. These fiction books are primarily for elementary school-age students although there are some young adult titles that could also be used in the upper grades and middle schools. Within this bibliography, specific autobiographies, biographies, or videos are listed for your use.

The Selected Bibliography of Authors also offers additional sources on multicultural literature, especially general bibliographical references, and provides references for beginning or extending your knowledge and skills on the writing process and writers workshop.

Appendix 2, Places of Birth and Birthdays for Authors, is for your use throughout the year if you wish to have a focus author each month or if you wish to include the authors from this book in your recognition of multicultural authors as models for your students.

Acknowledgments

This book is dedicated to young writers who take part in classroom writers workshops. I would like to thank Boise State University, with appreciation for services of the Curriculum Resource Center. Likewise, the staff of Boise Public Library Youth Services answered countless questions that kept this project moving forward. Angela Sue Mei Lee and Karla Swiggum, graduate assistants, helped with accuracy of multicultural titles and authors. Authors of multicultural children's literature gave of their time and good will, in interviews by phone, e-mail, or letter, graciously sharing their worlds with all of us. I thank them for their contributions. Teachers who came to my courses in children's literature or creative writing helped me clarify connections between writing and modeling on the best literature available. Professor Leona Manke of Albertson College of Idaho and teachers Cliff Yeary and Barry and Claire Laurance reviewed drafts. And all the folks at Scarecrow Press turned the final draft into a finished book. Much applause to all of them. Finally, I would like to thank my husband, Jeff, who supplied me with a mantra that works, of course, for all writers: "Just keep writing."

PERMISSIONS

Preface

"I Watched an Eagle Soar" from *Dancing Teepees: Poems of American Indian Youth*. Reprinted with permission from Virgina Driving Hawk Sneve, ©1989.

Artistic statement for Shonto Begay's paintings and prints reprinted with permission from Shonto Begay.

Excerpt from *Something about the Author*, edited by Anne Commire. Reprinted by permission of The Gale Group, © 1990.

Excerpt from *Flying with the Eagle, Racing the Great Bear* by Joseph Bruchac. Published and reprinted with permission of Joseph Bruchac and Troll Communications L.L.C., © 1993 by Joseph Bruchac.

Chapter 1

Excerpt from an interview conducted by David Weich with Christopher Paul Curtis at powells.com (Portland, Oregon) on April 5, 2000. Reprinted by permission of Powells.

Chapter 2

Excerpt from "Allen Say: Interview" by Martha Davis Beck. Reprinted with permission of Martha Davis Beck for *Riverbank Review*.

Excerpt from *High Elk's Treasure*. Reprinted with permission from Virginia Driving Hawk Sneve.

Chapter 3

Excerpt from *Anansi Goes Fishing* by Eric A. Kimmel. Reprinted by permission of Holiday House, Inc.

Excerpt from Allen Say's Caldecott Medal acceptance speech as it appeared in *The Horn Book Magazine*. Reprinted with permission from Allen Say.

Excerpt from *Mississippi Bridge* by Mildred D. Taylor, pictures by Max Ginsburg. Used with permission of Dial Books for Young Readers, an imprint of Penguin Putnam Books for Young Readers, a division of Penguin Putnam, Inc.

Excerpt from *The Fun House*. Reprinted with permission from Baymax Productions, Burbank, Calif., and Norma Sadler.

Chapter 4

Excerpt from *Jimmy Yellow Hawk,* © 1972, Holiday House. Reprinted with permission from Virginia Driving Hawk Sneve.
Excerpt from *Hershel and the Hanukkah Goblins* by Eric A. Kimmel. Reprinted by permission of Holiday House, Inc.

Chapter 5

From the *Mildred D. Taylor Penguin Putnam Catalog Biography.* Used with permission of Penguin Putnam Books for Young Readers, a division of Penguin Putnam, Inc., © 2000.
Excerpt from *My Name Is María Isabel* by Alma Flor Ada. Reprinted with permission of Atheneum Books for Young Readers, an imprint of Simon & Schuster Children's Publishing Division, © 1993 Alma Flor Ada.
Excerpt from *The Rooster Who Went to His Uncle's Wedding* by Alma Flor Ada. Used by permission of G. P. Putnam's Sons, a division of Penguin Putnam, Inc., © 1993 by Alma Flor Ada.

Chapter 6

Excerpt from *The First Strawberries: A Cherokee Story* by Joseph Bruchac. Used by permission of Penguin Putnam Inc., © 1993 by Joseph Bruchac.

Chapter 7

Excerpt from *Something about the Author*, edited by Anne Commire. Reprinted with permission of The Gale Group, © 1990.

Chapter 8

Excerpt from *The Butterfly Pyramid*. Reprinted with permission of Margarita González-Jensen and the Wright Group/McGraw-Hill, 1-800-523-2371.
Excerpt from "Five Questions: Katherine Paterson," in *Writers Digest*. Reprinted with permission of Sonya Haskins.

CHAPTER 1

Why Teach Literary Elements?

Fictional stories have conventions called *literary elements*. It's important to understand how to teach these elements when we teach creative writing in fictional genres because these elements are the underlying structure for the writing of fiction. They make up the "craft of fiction." One way to get a grasp of how literary elements work in stories is to look at the "rules" or "conventions" of verbal and nonverbal communication that we use to talk with each other.

Both verbal and nonverbal communication work because the rules we use to talk and listen allow us to be able to start, stop, or hesitate in a conversation. Conventions let us change our minds in mid-sentence, run our hands through our hair, scratch our heads, bob our heads up and down, shrug our shoulders, beckon someone, or even walk away. For the most part, all of us are understood. We have learned how to engage in verbal and nonverbal discourse because we want to understand others or we want ourselves to be understood by others.

The same needs and wants for us to be able to express ourselves well in verbal and nonverbal communication hold true in the written fictional world where we use the tools of the trade of fiction writing—literary elements—to make what we want to say understood. With those elements, writers communicate "story" to "audience," and show that they (the writers) understand who the readers are. The readers then bring their own perceptions, cultural connections, and understanding of how stories are "supposed" to work to the particular story being read.

LITERARY ELEMENTS STRUCTURE STORIES

Fictional genres—whether short stories, chapter books for middle grades, or novels, consist of literary elements in a particular format. Those elements—character, setting, plot, point of view, tone, theme, and style—are the "conventions" that writers use to "craft" narratives or stories. The conventions make sense for young writers to learn so that they can construct stories that are believable and predictable for their readers. The literary elements are the building blocks for oral or written stories.

Writers need to know and be able to use literary elements in the writing of fiction. In addition, in classrooms throughout this country, students are now asked to create narratives that include literary elements. They may be assessed on these narratives via "writing trait" rubrics.[1]

DEFINITIONS

While using this book, you could place brief definitions of literary elements of fiction writing on posters or large cards up in your classroom for student use. But before doing so, *wait a minute*. It is important to consider how you will introduce definitions of elements. The goal is not to have students just learn abstract terms about writing, but be able to know and use them to write fictional pieces of their own.

USING CONCRETE EXAMPLES FOR ABSTRACT TERMS

For younger children, writing a definition with a sentence and a picture that shows each element might be more appropriate. For example for "setting," you could cut out pictures from a magazine, showing day and night with the word *setting* printed above them, the pictures below with the labels *day* and *night* printed on the pictures.

INTRODUCING THREE ELEMENTS

Introducing the first three elements ("character," "setting," and "plot") can be easy to do. Consider the following literary elements for classroom use: character (Who is in the story?), setting (When and where does the story take place?), and plot (What happens in the story?). This is a way to introduce three elements briefly before using the strategies from the text.

FROM TELLING STORIES TO WRITING STORIES

Margarita González-Jensen, author of *The Butterfly Pyramid*, has family who came to the United States from Mexico. She makes it clear that in her culture, everyone told stories:

> Everybody in my family told stories. They would say, "Your grandfather did this." Or maybe my great aunt would tell about a battle in Mexico. They told the stories when I was young in San Antonio, to connect to our family.[2]

This next activity will give students exposure to seeing, hearing, and talking about literary elements through a discussion of story. Place the following questions on the board.

- Does anyone in your family tell stories? Who? When?
- Who are the people in the stories?
- Where does the story take place?
- What happens in the story?

Ask students to respond, and place some of their answers on the board. Then you might place the words *Character*, *Setting*, and *Plot* next to the answers to the questions. Placing the words with definitions on posters, as mentioned earlier, will give students a permanent visual to review terms.

A variety of strategies that you can use—pick and choose from—to meet your curricular needs are in this book. Authors' comments, such as the one below, can reinforce students' interest in writing.

> Question: "What advice do you have for young writers?"
> Paul Goble: "Read good books. Love your favorite books and reread them again and again. You don't have to be a writer. Only a few people end up writing, but if you want to write, work at it!"[3]

As you consider what books to use with the strategies in this book, it's important that the books be inclusive, that a wide variety of multicultural authors, male and female, be included. Diverse and authentic works of children's literature and the authors of those works will become the sources and models for student writing.

While the chapters in this book may focus on one or more elements, they can be used in sequence or in any order that meets your goals in a writing workshop. Many of the activities could be mini-lessons, as demonstrated in this chapter.

Merging reading and writing with literary elements is clearly presented in articles such as Marie Dionesio's "Responding to Literary Elements through Mini-lessons and Dialogue Journals,"[4] Mini-lessons and dialogue journals offer additional ways of increasing student understanding and writing about literary elements, even in the primary grades.

JOURNALS AND NOTES: GATHERING IDEAS FOR STORIES

Writers write from what they know. Laurence Yep explains how a relative from his childhood growing up as a Chinese boy in California shows up in one of his novels:

> Question: "Are there any people from your childhood in California that have turned into characters for your fictional stories?"
>
> Laurence Yep: "My grandmother and her tiny studio apartment are in *Child of the Owl*."[5]

Young writers can keep track of people, places, and events that may generate story ideas.

To encourage students to jot down ideas for future stories, you could have them create reading/writing logs or journals for gathering ideas for writing. My journals and notebooks are a pot-pourri of ideas—small sketches, crossouts, paragraphs, poems, and many, many beginnings. Journals may be used in a variety of ways:

Reading Log. Students record pages read under daily reading, and briefly in one or two sentences describe what they read.

Double Entry Log or Journal. Students write down something from a story—it could be character, setting, plot, point of view, tone, theme, or style—on the left side. On the right side, students write their own reactions, feelings, thoughts to the quote or sentences written. Questions you might ask students are:

- What do you think about it?
- How does it make you feel?
- Are there any questions about what you read?
- What are they?

Vocabulary Log. Students write down vocabulary words from stories that they think would be great to know. They find one word each day in their reading and write the sentence that contains it, underline the word, and then write what it means in their own words, still relating it to the story.

Character Log. Students make lists of whomever they wish from the stories who are characters they would want to know. Why would they want to know them?

Story Resolution Logs. Students write titles of stories that they read, and tell how the story ended, and what the title had to do with the story.

AUTHORS AND THEIR CRAFT

What authors do, how they craft their works, and why they do write what they write are questions answered by authors in this book. For instance, when Walter Dean Myers, an African American writer, talks about his style of writing, he emphasizes how challenging it is to be clear to reach all readers. He is committed to reaching a wide audience for his books:

> Question: "Looking back over your writing career, what has been the most challenging part of writing that you have had to deal with when you write?"
>
> Walter Dean Myers: "I've always wanted to write as clearly as possible, and simply enough to be accessible to a wide audience of poor readers, and yet I want to use as much of the traditional writer's arsenal as possible. The balance of these concepts has been a challenge which I still enjoy."[6]

Each chapter illuminates particular cultures of authors through their "voices" as they give advice to young writers or talk about specific literary elements. For example, how does a writer decide what character will tell the story? As an African American who grew up in Flint, Michigan, Christopher Paul Curtis talks about how he figured out this literary element for *Bud, Not Buddy*:

> I don't outline my stories. I don't know where it's going to be. Originally, my grandfather was the ten-year-old orphan in the story. I don't feel comfortable with it until I get a narrator, then the narrator starts to talk and I go from there. Well, he turned out to be this ten-year-old orphan, Bud.[7]

To encourage choice in the books that you use, many authors are included in this book. It is, unfortunately, not inclusive of all the fine writers of children's literature, but all writers have been chosen to promote the use of cultural perspectives in literary elements by young writers in their own writing.

CHAPTER 2

Who: Writing the Characters in a Story

As young writers consider what their stories will be about, they need to answer the question: Who will be the character or characters in my story? These stories have a character or characters who are involved in a series of events. What reporters do when they write stories for newspapers is similar to what fiction writers have to do to make their stories work. Reporters for newspapers and television are aware that events don't exist in a vacuum, that real people cause them or are affected by them. And to get to the people and the events, reporters are trained in questioning techniques. They use them to pull a story out of events that tumble around us. They focus on such questions as: Who? What? How? Where? When? Why?

Writers of fiction ask those same questions and the answers to those questions give us the main literary elements of a story:

- Who? Character(s)
- What and How? Plot and Subplots
- Where and When? The Setting (includes time and place, individual scenes)
- Why? Character Motivation

The last question of "why" is not necessarily included in newspaper articles and television reporting. The motivation and reason for something happening is something we, the readers, of the news stories want to know, but that may or may not be answered in the article. But we read anyway because we want to know what happened to the people in the article. But why the house caught fire or why the child who won a contest entered the winning work in the first place might not be known. And as much as reporters want to know the answers to questions of what motivates people to do what they do and hunt for the "human interest" part of the story, they may not be able to find the answer or answers to these questions for a particular newsworthy story.

In fiction, however, the motivations for what characters do and why they do what they do must be there. They are crucial as to whether or not we believe the story, or suspend disbelief to go with the author, who speaks through a narrator in the story. Rather than reading a news piece, where readers would get a glimpse of people and events and then move on to another section of the paper, readers in literature do not separate themselves from the story. They identify with characters and move right along with them through the story over a longer period of time.

Writers, engaged in the craft of fiction, create and "tell" readers why characters do what they do" through characters' thoughts, speech, or actions and through the story narration as well. To have students be able to understand "character," you could use essential pieces of information from the list below. Character "facts" are woven into the activities later in the chapter.

- Characters may be a person, animals, or objects.
- Characters are revealed by thoughts, speech (dialogue), or actions.
- Characters are revealed by statements, questions, and exclamations.
- Characters are revealed by silence.
- Characters are revealed by giggles, pauses, yells, or sighs.
- Characters are revealed by nonverbal communication, including acts that they engage in with others, such as taking part in sports and the like.
- Characters are also defined by their role in the story. For a story to work, a "character" engages in some action in some defined role in a story. The character may be a person or a "personified animal," who in some ways might speak like a person, or act like a person or dress like a person as in folktales or fantasies. Or a character might be an object, such as a toy or doll. In addition, a character is revealed through the story by action, speech, description of appearance or illustrations of appearance, narrative description by others in the story, or by the author's own words.

MORE ABOUT SPEECH

Most importantly, speech, with its conventions of grammar, sentence structure, intonation, and inflection, must appear in a written story, just as the starting, stopping, and hesitating that we hear in all conversations could be shown as part of an oral story. Again, though, the written conventions of speech and ways to show nonverbal communication through description and action mean that writers have to give readers enough information to understand their characters and why they do what they do when they do it.

LAYOUTS FOR CHARACTER VISUALS

The following table shows different characters in different books to assist with the identification of character. A sample table on the chalkboard or computer can assist students with the understanding of the *identification* of character.

Story	Character	Person, animal, or object
The Great Gilly Hopkins	eleven-year-old girl	person
Bud, Not Buddy	ten-year-old boy	person
Year of Impossible Goodbyes	ten-year-old girl	person
My Name Is María Isabel	young girl	person
Sam and the Tigers	young boy	person
The Story of Jumping Mouse	a mouse	animal
Anansi Goes Fishing	a spider, turtle	animals
Too Much Talk	a king's throne	object
Winnie-the-Pooh	a bear-toy	object
The Adventures of Pinocchio	a wooden puppet/young boy	object/person
Anansi and the Moss-Covered Rock	a rock	object that can knock animals down
Iktomi and the Boulder	boulder	object

Once students are able to identify the characters in a story and whether they are persons, animals, or objects, then they can take a look at what the character says (speech) and does (actions or behavior) and the motivations for that speech or action. Then students can develop stories with characters who show what they do and why they do it. The idiom "action speaks louder than words" reflects fictional reality as well as the world we actually live in. A simple list can also give students a spatial view of what characters say and do in stories and be made into a large chart posted in the room for students to add information to from the stories they read. The list can include these entries:

- Character
- Thoughts
- Speech
- Actions
- Appearance/traits
- What others say about the characters
- What is shown in pictures

To figure out "character," you need to know the above. Writers, such as Eric Kimmel, know that without character, you don't have story. He goes to his own cultural background and childhood experiences for some of the characters who show up in his stories:

> Question: "Are there any people from your childhood that have turned into characters for your books?"
>
> Eric Kimmel: "There definitely are, but frequently it's not the exact person that I use but that person's way of reacting or understanding the world. The best example is the character of Bubba Brayna in *The Chanukkah Guest*. She's based on my grandma. She loved animals, especially big dogs. She would not have been afraid of a bear. I could see her laughing the whole episode off as I wrote the story. The aspect of nearsightedness came from Mr. Magoo cartoons, which I loved as a child."[1]

Characters can also be defined by what they do or how they act in a story. This way of looking at character helps students understand such concepts as tension, conflict, a problem, and a solution. It gives them the reason for why the characters exist in the first place, and in that disclosure, we see the motivation for the words, action, and movement of the characters in the story. While there are several different character types ranging from simple or flat to complex or round, the most often seen in children's literature are those that could be labeled flat or round.

ROUND CHARACTERS

The main character (protagonist) is usually a round character in a children's story, as one who is most fully developed in terms of characterization. This character has a problem and solves it. This is the character with whom the reader identifies. A young writer must figure out how to convey the character in such a way that his or her audience/imaginary reader can say I know, I understand this character, and I am willing to go along with this character in this story.

AND IN THE OTHER CORNER . . .

What or who opposes the main character is known as the "antagonist"—connected to the cause of a problem for the main character. The antagonist may be a fully rounded character, one who is in opposition to the main character and tries to keep the main character from getting what he or she wants or needs. An antagonist might also be the environment or natural world that keeps the main character from getting what he or she wants or needs, which might be physical survival.

A list like the one below may provide students a way to clarify two basic kinds of characters and help them understand the relationships between them.

- Main character or antagonist, or character opposite to main character
- Kind (flat or round)
- Example to show kind

Once writers understand that characters are different "types," or kinds, they can figure out how to convey who the characters are and what they do. Unfortunately, "show, don't tell," an idiomatic expression, is often used in the teaching of creative writing. But the statement, which is meant to emphasize that showing through action is more important than telling what happens in narrative, is misleading to students. Students may see it as meaning no telling, or "no talking" in the story, or no relating of things that happened, and that is far from what is meant. The best stories make use of dialogue both telling us what happened through action, and telling us what happened through narrative. Weaving *telling* and *showing* together gives us the "big picture" of what is happening. Dialogue and action, description, and narration are all important parts of the story, keeping us in the beat of the story while giving us information to understand the character and events taking place. What is important is that young writers need to create characters who do talk and act; they need to give the characters the burden of the story so that the characters carry the weight, allowing the reader to take part in the story and go through what the characters go through.

A character doesn't exist in a vacuum, separate from the plot of a story. He or she has some problem to overcome and he or she seeks to control events to solve that problem. The concern with events within the story structure leads us to plot construction. Although plot and character are inseparable in a story, they may be quite separate as we begin structuring a story by asking such questions as "Who does what when?" But each of us writes differently. Some of us think of characters, then place them in a plot construction with a problem to solve; some think of plot and then come up with the characters who will be in the story. Some of us, when we write, think of both character and plot so close together that we are not aware of which came first.

I thought about one idea for over thirty years before it became "The Fun House," a short story. That the main characters would be children, two cousins who go to the amusement park on the first day of its opening in spring and go through a fun house, a fantasy place, were ideas that came much later.

There are no hard-and-fast rules for how a writer designs or crafts characters or plots, only that certain elements of character and plot must be in stories for the stories to work at all.

THE POWER OF PICTURES WITH STORY TEXT

For student writers in your classrooms, an understanding of the power of pictures to convey story is as important as understanding how characters work in story text. Students need to know that multicultural writers who are both the authors and illustrators for their own picture storybooks create books that integrate story, of which characters are a part, in both text and illustration. Other authors of the story text in picture storybooks may not illustrate their own books. Regardless, whether one person or two create the book, the picture storybook must be one interconnected form.

Those who author and illustrate their own books work in many different ways to create plot and/or characters. Some write the text first, then draw the pictures; others create the illustrations and then the text. Allen Say sometimes has drawn the pictures first, then figured out the story.[2] We could say that he "plots" his watercolors, then creates the text to go along with them.

Young writers may wish to create pictures and then write the stories to go with them, using language experience approaches to becoming writers. In language experience activities, students create pictures, tell teachers what the pictures are about, and the teachers write down what students say because students can't yet write the structured way that they speak with the sentence patterns they use orally. Telling their stories with pictures gives younger students a way to engage in storytelling. You might ask students to record a story via tape player or computer, using the computer for creating pictures.

COMING UP WITH CHARACTERS

How do authors of multicultural literature come up with the characters for their stories? Eric Kimmel goes to his childhood for ideas. Like Eric Kimmel, Joseph Bruchac creates his stories with many of the relatives and people from his childhood. They have appeared in his autobiography, *Bowman's Store*, and a series of other stories about his childhood:

> But they've also inspired, influenced, and been incorporated into fictional characters. Great-Grama Bowman in *Fox Song* has a lot in common with

my grandparents and also Swift Eagle—who once told me that the fox was his special animal and that I should look for it to show itself after he had passed away. (And, indeed, that happened, though not when I was a little boy, but on my fortieth birthday.) Bits of dialogue, character traits, little things that real people have done and said appear in my books often. Sometimes I'm very aware of it and other times I only realize it later.[3]

Obviously though, writers write what they know from their own pasts, and what they don't know, they imagine and figure out.

Getting students to see their own ethnic backgrounds as places where stories dwell can lead them to ideas for characters. To recognize and value themselves, their pasts, and their backgrounds and traditions is an important part of understanding themselves as writers.

Virginia Driving Hawk Sneve grew up in South Dakota. People from her childhood appear in her books:

Question: "Are there any people from your Sioux childhood on the Rosebud reservation that have turned into characters for your fictional stories?"

Virginia Driving Hawk Sneve: "In *When Thunders Spoke*, the grandfather was based on my own paternal grandfather, who was very traditional and worried that young people were forgetting their Indian heritage. The storekeeper was inspired by several white merchants in border towns who exploited the Indians."[4]

For Margarita González-Jensen, the characters and plot for *The Butterfly Pyramid* came out of her own experience with her son on a vacation in Cancun, Mexico:

Question: "How did you come up with the characters and plot in *The Butterfly Pyramid*?"

Margarita González-Jensen: "I went to Cancun with my son Roger, who was five, and went to a store and bought him a butterfly net. He used that butterfly net to catch fish, and everything else, but never for a butterfly because there wasn't even *one* around. The net disappeared—broken or whatever. In one of those open-air rental Volkswagens, we headed toward a pyramid on a jungle path. All of sudden butterflies were everywhere. We held them. We knew we were witnessing a migration. I thought about that later, that something about it would make it a neat story. I wanted to write about a little boy who had a special relationship with his mother."[5]

Walter Dean Myers draws many of his characters from "real" childhood friends:

> Question: "Are there any people from your childhood that have turned into characters for your fictional stories?"
>   Walter Dean Myers: "In *Fast Sam, Cool Clyde & Stuff*, fully half of the characters (Binky, Light Billy, Carnation Charlie) were actual childhood friends. I often use real people as characters and change the names in the final draft."[6]

What Myers does is to "see" real people as his characters. He is one writer who draws from what and who he knows while writing to clearly be able to see his characters in his stories. Students can create characters from people they know and change the names to create the "fictional" world they need for their stories.

CHARACTER STRATEGIES

Journal Activities: Major and Minor Characters

Major Characters. Have students choose a character from your read-aloud (a picture storybook, chapter book, or novel). Tell them to focus just on that character as you are reading. After you have finished reading a chapter or the book, ask them to list character traits or descriptors for their character and give an example from the book that shows the trait of their character. Students may record these traits in their journals or you may place them on posterboards in the room under the horizontal label *Title, Character, Traits, Examples from book*.
Minor Characters. Minor characters are important. Give the following directions to students:

1. Pick out a minor character from one of the stories and write one sentence in your journal that explains why that character is in the story.
2. Imagine that you are a minor character, such as in a story that you have heard.

3. Write in your journal your reaction to three events of the story as if you are that minor character. Your first sentence may be "I am. . . ."
4. In small groups, share your sentences and your reactions as minor characters to three events in the story.
5. Tell the rest of your group why your minor character is important to the story.

Journal Activity. Students may keep literary journals (they can design their own covers) and designate one page for each book they read. A title for each book is placed at the top of the page as they listen to a story or read one on their own. They list one character and write in their own words one or two phrases or sentences about the character.

Just Imagine

Directions for students: Imagine that a character from a story you've read is walking through the door right now. Directions for teachers: Ask students:

- What does he or she look like?
- What would he or she say?
- How would he or she say it?

Which Character Are You?

These suggestions are for use with a book that is familiar to everyone in the class or for use in literature circle groups in which students all read the same book and engage in reading/writing activities with it. Possible characters from books may be listed on the board. Students pick a character from one of the books/authors listed or others of your choice.

Directions for students: Pretend that you are a character from a story. Tell about yourself to the class without identifying who you are. The class will have to guess who you are. You will call on your classmates to identify the character or tell who the character is by name. The following is a list of books for use with this activity: For K–3 students:

Ada, Alma Flor. *My Name Is María Isabel.*
Bruchac, Joseph. *Fox Song.*

De San Souci, Robert. *The Talking Eggs*.
Hoffman, Mary. *Amazing Grace*.
Kimmel, Eric. *I Took My Frog to the Library*.
Kimmel, Eric. *Anansi and the Moss-Covered Rock*.
Kimmel, Eric. *Anansi Goes Fishing*.
Lester, Julius. *Sam and the Tigers*.
Paterson, Katherine. *The Tale of the Mandarin Ducks*.
Say, Allen. *A River Dream*.
Soto, Gary. *The Cat's Meow*.
Soto, Gary. *Chato's Kitchen*.
Yep, Laurence. *The Dragon Prince: A Chinese Beauty and the Beast Tale*.

For 4–6 students:

Curtis, Christopher Paul. *Bud, Not Buddy*.
Ho, Minfong. *The Clay Marble*.
Hurmence, Belinda. *A Girl Called Boy*.
Myers, Walter Dean. *Me, Mop, and the Moondance Kid*.
Myers, Walter Dean. *Won't Know Until I Get There*.
Paterson, Katherine. *Jip: His Own Story*.
Paterson, Katherine. *The Great Gilly Hopkins*.
Paterson, Katherine. *Come Sing, Jimmy Jo*.
Soto, Gary. *Summer on Wheels*.
Tate, Eleanora E. *The Secret of Gumbo Grove*.
Taylor, Mildred. *Roll of Thunder, Hear My Cry*.
Yep, Laurence. *Thief of Hearts*.

Guess Who?

This is a written variation of the character activity described above using a particular book that all students in the class, literature circle, or book club have read.

Directions for students: Using one of the characters in the book, write a first-person description so that others in the class have to guess who it is. Finish your paragraphs with "Who am I?"

On note cards, students write down who they think the character is. Each "character" calls on classmates to guess who the character is. Written note cards with character names are a check for character identification.

Writing a Character Letter: Dear?

Using Alma Flor Ada's *Dear Peter Rabbit* and *Yours Truly, Goldilocks*, ask students to write a letter from one character to another. Using variants of the same tale, such as *The Three Little Pigs*, have students write as if they are one nursery rhyme character writing to another. For example, one of the pigs in *The Three Javelinas* could write to another of the pigs in one of the other stories, the wolf, or another nursery rhyme character altogether. The sample table heads below gives students ideas for describing various characters:

Title	Character	Trait(s)

Younger students can record their letters on tape or onto a voice-programmed computer disk. They could also draw pictures and explain the pictures.

Comparison Activity with Character: On TV or in the Movies

First, students name a favorite character from a book read aloud or on their own. Students then list the traits of that person. They then think of a TV show or movie that has a character who has the same trait, such as greedy or kind. They can list the movie character next to the book character, the trait, and how the trait is shown in the book and film.

Small-Group Work: How Do You See Characters in Stories?

Directions for students: First, pick a character from a story you have read. On a small rectangle of paper, write one trait of your character (inner trait) and then write words to describe whether your character is a boy or girl; what your character looks like (appearance), such as eye color, hair color, and hair style; or any other description from the story, whether in words or pictures. Second, find a picture of a person, an animal, or an object from magazines that you think shows your character.

Third, read the description and show your picture. Explain why the picture could show the character in your story.

Identifying Types of Characters

Semantic Feature Chart. Down one side of a sheet of paper, list the characters in the story. Across the top, write "flat" or "round." Have students place a check in the correct column for the character.

Identifying and Defining Character Types. Make a list of the characters from any of the multicultural books that you have read aloud or that students have read on their own. Place the title on the board, overhead, or computer, and ask students to list the characters. Then create a simple table with the following heads:

Type (flat or round)   Why?   What makes them flat or round?

Focus on Folktale Characters

Using a variety of folktales from many cultures, have students identify the characters and explain one trait that they have.

Character Traits: Trickster Tales/Cleverness

Because Eric Kimmel's books contain "trickster" characters, they are perfect for this activity. His words that follow could be used with those books:

> A lot of my stories are about witches, goblins, tricksters. I retell stories from around the world. I think a lot of that comes from the fact that I grew up in New York City, where you're surrounded by people from all over the world. Also, when you're growing up in a big city, you learn to look out for yourself. Don't assume that everyone is your friend or that they have your best interests at heart. Hustlers, bums, con artists — they're all part of the landscape. I grew up loving that human panorama. I used to take the subway up to Times Square every weekend just to watch the show. Broadway was at its peak, but I'll tell you, the best show was going on in the street outside the theaters. And the best part was — it was free![7]

Have students choose one character—a "trickster"—in a folktale. The following is a list of possible tales to use. For grades K–3:

Aardema, Verna. *Oh, Kojo! How Could You! An Ashanti Tale*.
Aardema, Verna. *Rabbit Makes a Monkey Out of Lion*.
Aardema, Verna. *Borreguita and the Coyote*.
Ho, Minfong. *Brother Rabbit: A Cambodian Tale*.
Kimmel, Eric. *Anansi and the Moss-Covered Rock*.
Kimmel, Eric. *Hershel and the Hanukkah Goblins*.
Lester, Julius, reteller. *Uncle Remus: The Complete Tales*.
McDermott, Gerald. *Raven: A Trickster Tale from the Northwest*.

For grades 4–6:

Bruchac, Joseph. *The Rainbow People*.
Bruchac, Joseph. *Stone Giants and Flying Heads: Adventure Stories of the Iroquois*.
Goble, Paul. *Iktomi and the Boulder* or *Iktomi and the Ducks*, or other "Iktomi" stories.

In a large- or small-group discussion, ask students to identify how the character is clever or can trick others. Have students then create trickster stories with a coyote, spider, Iktomi, or other character who outwits another or is outwitted. Students can share their trickster stories in small groups or with the whole class, and then place them in a book entitled *Trickster Stories*.

Word Webs

With students in younger grades, in the center of the board place a main character's name. Draw lines from the character's name and place words to tell about that character as strands from the center. Students give reasons aloud why that word fits that character. Older students can work on their own or with partners to create the web and discuss their reasons for the description strands.

Characterization: Writing a Character

The kinds of answers that students choose for the questions as they work through the characterization outline help to determine the eventual makeup of the character—what he or she would think, say, and do in a story. Directions for students: Imagine that you are a character searching for a part in a story. For the author to be able to include you in his or her story, the author needs to know a lot about you. As a character, write down as much information about yourself as possible:

What is your name?
How old are you?
Where do you live?
What is your ethnic background?
What are the features of your face (such as eyes, hair, nose, mouth)?
How do you look to other people?
What kinds of clothes do you wear?
What kinds of clothes do you want to wear?
What do you like to do?
What don't you like to do?
If you are in school, what do you do there?
What do you do at home?
What do you do on weekends?
What kinds of food do you like?
What kinds of food don't you like?
How athletic are you?
What do you worry about most?
How much traveling do you do?
Where do you go?
What do you like to do when you travel?
What is your favorite food?
Where do you find it?
What is your favorite drink?
What is your favorite kind of music?
Do you play a musical instrument?
What are your friends like?

What do you do with your friends?

What kinds of people don't you like?

Do you walk or bicycle, take a bus, or drive to where you want to go?

Name two friends who might get along with a "character" like yourself and tell what they are like.

Note: The next step would be to take each of these additional characters through the above steps to see what each is like. Then students can ask what kinds of characters wouldn't get along with the main character and for what reasons. This activity begins the "plotting" of a story.

You can also use art to help students develop their character in writing. Give students magazine pictures showing ordinary people or animals in unusual settings or engaged in some action. Each student chooses a picture or photo and is asked to turn this person or animal into a character for a story. These visuals can be used to talk about what the person or animal looks like and what they are doing in the picture. Pictures or photos are placed on the wall, and students read their descriptions. Others in the class tell which picture matches the description and why.

Connections between Characters in Books and People in the Real World

Reality and imagination come together when a writer creates a story. Use Gary Soto's words to show that connection:

Question: "Are there any people from your childhood that have turned into characters for your fictional stories?"

Gary Soto: "My fiction for young people is stuff of the imagination. One exception is Jesse, a YA novel set during *el movimiento* of the United Farm Workers. I am the character Jesse, a first-year community college student; but then again, some of the characteristics that make up Jesse's personality are imaginative. I think most writers will write one or two autobiographical novels, then move on to material that may have some biographical moments but mostly will be true fiction. This is what I have discovered about my work. My novels *Taking Sides* and *Pacific Crossing*, for instance, are creative inventions. I am not anything like the protagonist Lincoln Mendoza."[8]

Here is a question for you to ask students: "Do characters in books remind us of real people, other children, parents, brother or sisters, or friends whom we know?" Using the following books or others with characters (children, animals, objects, or adults), ask students which character reminds them of themselves or reminds them of other people they know. How or why? Students can write sentences or paragraphs that explain their choices. Then, as a group, students can give their choices to the teacher to create big list of choices for characters. For grades K–3:

Ada, Alma Flor. *The Gold Coin.*
Paterson, Katherine. *Celia and the Sweet, Sweet Water.*
San Souci, Robert D. *The Talking Eggs: A Folktale from the American South.*
Say, Allen. *Emma's Rug.*

For grades 4–6:

Paterson, Katherine. *Bridge to Terabithia.*
Sneve, Virginia Driving Hawk. *Jimmy Yellow Hawk.*
Tate, Eleanora E. *Thank You, Dr. Martin Luther King.*
Taylor, Mildred. *Roll of Thunder, Hear My Cry.*

Story Quilt

Read a fictional story that has the quilt as an object of importance, such as:

Flournoy, Valerie. *The Patchwork Quilt.* Illustrated by Jerry Pinkney.
Guback, Georgia. *Luka's Quilt* (Hawaiian).
Hopkinson, Deborah. *Sweet Clara and the Freedom Quilt.*
Polacco, Patricia. *The Keeping Quilt.*

Have students make paper squares. Divide the squares on the diagonal with a line so that the name of the character is on one side of the line and the picture is on the other side of the line. Glue the pieces together to show characters' names and scenes. Extra squares can be colored to reflect a color that they would find in the story.

Characters in Illustration in Picture Storybooks

After you have read a multicultural picture storybook (one with both text and pictures) or students have read one on their own, have students choose an illustration to review. Ask students to respond to the following questions:

- Who are two characters in this story?
  What do they look like? (physical features)
  What do they do? (actions and behavior)
  Why do they do what they do?
  How do you know what makes them do what they do?
  From the pictures, what do they need?
  From the pictures, what makes them do what they do?
  What is one thing about these characters that you see in both the printed story and the illustration?

Cartoons to Show Speech and Thought of Characters

Have a stick-figure drawing of two characters showing what is being said as compared to what is being thought. Have students bring in cartoons and talk about who the characters in the cartoons are. Ask students the following questions:

- What are they saying?
  How do you know?
- What are they thinking?
  How do you know?
- What are they doing?
  How do you know?

Discuss with the students how pictures can show action and explain that in print, when there are no pictures, each reader or listener creates his or her own picture. It is up to the writer to provide the pictures through words for the reader.

Grammar: Oral Work with Identifying Quotation Marks/Tag Lines

Do characters sound like real people talking? Students need to understand how conventions of speech show up in writing. "Tag lines" or indicators for speech involve the use of "said" and other words such as "yelled," "whispered," and so on. To identify tag lines, have students give you sentences and place them on the board, overhead, or computer.

Using names of students in the class, show students how to place the quotation marks to indicate who said what. Then have students identify the tag lines from multicultural fiction books that include dialogue. Note that some books use quotation marks and some do not. Also, note that our voices change as we read aloud; our voices shift as we go from dialogue or speech in story to tag lines.

Grammar: Writing of Quotation Marks and Narrative Tag Lines

Using a variety of multicultural books, ask students to complete the following:

- Add a line of dialogue to a character's dialogue in the story.
- Write original dialogue for a character from the story.
- Create and write dialogue for a character that you have made up, using tag lines and quotation marks correctly.
- Make tag lines with quotation marks for characters' words to show different patterns.
  1. The dialogue would be first, then either the name of the character or "he said" or "she said."
     Example: "I want to go to the top of the mountain," Jill said.
     Example: "I want to go to the top of the mountain," she said.
  2. Some dialogue would be first, then the character name and the word "said," and then more dialogue.
     Example: "It might be hard to do," Jill said, "but I want to go to the top of the mountain."
  3. First would be the name of the character, then the word "said," then dialogue.
     Example: Jill said, "It might be hard, but I want to go to the top of the mountain."

Have students use other words besides "said" to show sounds and feelings. They could use *yelled, screamed, hollered, howled, whispered*. Students could also try out words such as *sighed, laughed, smiled*, or *frowned* to show feelings around dialogue.

Identifying a Character's Thoughts

Sometimes readers get to see a character's thoughts by words that the author uses such as *he/she wondered, she thought, he/she wanted to do something, he/she could see, he could tell*, or *he didn't know*. Virginia Driving Hawk Sneve's description of Joe High Elk in *High Elk's Treasure* shows us how he feels but also demonstrates his thoughts with the words "he could tell."

> Wet and cold, Joe sat hunched on his heels, hugging his knees and staring out of the mouth of the cave. The rain was still falling, but he could tell from the way the trees stood, quietly accepting the water, that the wind had died. The storm was almost over.[9]

Writing of a Character's Thoughts

Have students create a character—a person or an animal with a name. Then have them write and describe the character, giving the character's feelings and thoughts. The following will give you examples to use to give the students ideas:

Bruchac, Joseph. *Flying with the Eagle, Racing the Great Bear*.
Goble, Paul. *Iktomi and the Ducks*.

After students understand how to show thoughts and feelings, have them write thoughts and feelings of characters. It does not matter if feelings or thoughts are expressed first. But it is important that there be some description of the character. Give students the following story summary:

Your character, whether a person or an animal who is named, has just finished a race. It was a hard race to win because the character had never been in a race before. The temperature during the day was quite high, and the race took place at noon. Did the character win the race or not? If so, how does he or she feel, what does he or she think about it? If not, how does he or she feel, what does he or she think about it?

Cultural Connection with Dialect/Language

To make a story more authentic, authors may include another language or dialect. Authors such as Margarita González-Jensen and Shonto Begay understand the importance of one's native language becoming the connection to storytelling.

> Question: "Do you think/write your stories in Spanish first, then translate them into English?"
>
> Margarita González-Jensen: "I work in Spanish first in my mind. I am bilingual and I do my own translating. I use Spanish phrases in books published in English. For instance, the mother might say "come and eat" in Spanish, and I would work the English translation within the text, not immediately after it, but so that it would be hooked together for the reader, who might not know the language. That way the reader would be able to understand what was said."[10]

When Shonto Begay talks about the importance of Navaho to his storytelling, he shows us how important a first language can be in telling stories.

> Question: "How important is it for the native language you speak to be in your books and why?"
>
> Shonto Begay: "It's pretty important for my native language to be in my works. It is the language I grew up with, the language I heard in stories, the language in which I came to be who I am. I didn't learn English until I went to boarding schools."[11]

You could use the quotes above with students and then have students write a dialogue between two characters. One of the characters could speak some words in another language or a different dialect. Ask students to think of a few words in a language they can add to their story to enrich the cultural connection they are trying to make.

Books that offer dialects of English or other languages to add authenticity to the story include, for grades K–3:

Aardema, Verna. *Borreguita and the Coyote* (Spanish).

Aardema, Verna. *The Riddle of the Drum* (Spanish).

Begay, Shonto. *Ma'ii and Cousin Horned Toad* (Navaho).

Lester, Julius. *Sam and the Tigers: A New Telling of* Little Black Sambo (African American rural dialect).

McKissack, Patricia C. *Flossie and the Fox* (African American rural dialect).

Myers, Walter Dean. *Mr. Monkey and the Gotcha Bird* (original tale, rhythmic African and Caribbean dialects).

Soto, Gary. *Chato's Kitchen* (Spanish).

Soto, Gary. *Chato and the Party Animals* (Spanish).

Steptoe, John. *Uptown* (African American urban dialect).

Steptoe, John. *Stevie* (African American urban dialect).

For grades 4–6:

Bruchac, Joseph. *Flying with the Eagle, Racing the Great Bear* (Native American tribal languages).

Curtis, Christopher Paul. *Bud, Not Buddy* (African American urban dialect).

Kimmel, Eric. *Four Dollars and Fifty Cents* (Western).

San Souci, Robert D. *The Talking Eggs: A Folktale from the American South* (Creole).

Soto, Gary. *Baseball in April & Other Stories* (Spanish).

Soto, Gary. *Off and Running* (Spanish).

Taylor, Mildred D. Any of her books (African American rural dialect).

Assessment: Characterization

With a book that is familiar to all students, you can check your students' knowledge of characterization. Draw a circle on a piece of paper and section it into five parts: thoughts of, action of, speech of, from others in the story, and from the author. Ask students to fill in the chart and tell you what they know about the character from each of these ways to tell or show a character in a story. Fill in a sample, one for each part, using the familiar story for information. Each student uses a book that he or she has read and a character of his or her choice to fill in the charts. Students can discuss their characterization chart in small- or large-group format. Papers may be checked for accuracy of identification and understanding.

Dramatization: Characters Come to Life

Each student prepares a character description from a multicultural book, taking notes on what the character is like. He or she then creates a "Who am I?" chart and writes a story in which he or she is a main character who has come to life. As a character, the student stands silently. Then one by one, taking turns, each student "comes to life" by speaking as the "I" of the story. Finally, each student creates a self-character description to be read aloud to a group.

Art/Tactile Approach to Character Names/Grammar for the Capital "I"

With an alphabet cereal or food product, students can spell the names of a favorite character from a multicultural book in an interesting pattern. When a character is shown by "I" in the story, have students use only the "I" in their patterns to demonstrate that the "I" of the story is how we see the story told.

Assessment: Identification of Story Character Names/Traits

Using eight characters from a story read aloud, or a story that students have read on their own, have students match character names to traits. Place eight character names on eight slips of paper and eight personality traits for the characters on eight other slips of paper. In small groups, have students identify which character goes with which trait.

Writing Characters: Names, Traits, and Descriptions

All young writers need to be able to use the English language effectively to come up with characters that will take a reader through a story.

Eric Kimmel: My advice to students is to use your ears for interesting ways of using language. Think about descriptions. How would you describe a person who is friendly, beautiful, wicked so that your reader can clearly see that character? How do you describe heat, cold, hunger? Don't worry about being "authentic." Your job is to tell the story. A good story is a good story. Tell a good tale and the rest will fall into place.[12]

Students think of characters on their own. They write down their character's name, a trait that shows what the character is like in terms of personality, and one physical trait that the character has in terms of appearance or movement. Have multicultural books for them to browse through to get ideas.

Assessment: Writing the Character Description

With the information from "Writing Characters: Names, Traits, and Descriptions," students write a paragraph, with character name, appearance, internal traits, and so on. Here are some things they may consider: colors, clothes, the things they carry, their possessions. For other activities using colors, see chapter 7 and chapter 8.

Art and Character Portraits

Have students draw a portrait of a character as he or she appears in a story on one half of a piece of paper. Then have them use the other half to write words that tell about the character or what happens (events) in the story. Another option is that students can make a collage from magazine pictures to show their character in one of the events of the story.

CHAPTER 3

When and Where:
Setting (Place, Time, and Detail)

Once students have decided on a main character and have developed their character through characterization activities, they need to decide (if they haven't already) where their main character lives (place) and when (time). Place, time, and "scene" within place and time are parts of setting.

PLACE

Students from your classroom have experiences that consist of home, school, relatives' homes, friends' homes, stores, malls, parks, or play-grounds. But each student may have places that they go to or come from that are unique to them and their families—important sources of material for settings. Those particular settings also may be reflections of particular ethnic backgrounds.

TIME

For students, there are many real-world indicators of time: hour, minute, second, day, night, morning, afternoon, evening, yesterday, to-day, tomorrow, spring, summer, fall, winter, last year, this year, next year, and so on. Any of these could become the "time" of the story or be combined to more specifically describe setting, such as "tomorrow morning."

DETAIL

Sometimes determining a setting for a story may be simple, but to make a setting come alive, more detail may be necessary for the story being told. With a knowledge of how settings work in stories, students can create settings for their own stories that include place, time, and detail.

SIMPLE SETTINGS

One of the best sources for understanding simple settings is within the genre of folktales. Folktales have conventions about setting that give us a generalized time and place in story. Readers hear words in these folktales that give them "place" in a story. Words such as "near a river," "in a village," or "by the shores of a mountain lake" give a minimal description of setting. These "backdrop" settings don't have much detail.

Sometimes authors vary the setting as they tell a story in their own way. Eric Kimmel's retelling of *Anansi Goes Fishing* is accompanied by Janet Stevens's illustrations. Those illustrations are the perfect "backdrop" to hold us in time and place, but let the story really take over. *Anansi Goes Fishing*, which takes place in Africa, has specific time frames: "one fine afternoon" and "tomorrow." The story takes place "by the river."[1] In an interview, Eric Kimmel discusses the setting for this "Anansi" story.

> Question: "How did you figure out how to write the setting for *Anansi Goes Fishing?*"
>
> Eric Kimmel: "That wasn't difficult. *Anansi Goes Fishing*, like my other Anansi stories, is a folktale from West Africa. That's where most of the Anansi stories come from, either Africa or the West Indies. So on the one hand I begin with the assumption of an African setting. However, the story's real setting is Anansi-land. Setting isn't important in this story. What counts is the interaction between the characters and the fun of watching two hustlers trying to out-hustle each other. Janet Stevens, the illustrator, understands this perfectly. She puts her patio furniture, sunglasses, Hawaiian shirt into the pictures. There's a vague 'jungle' setting, but it's more a movie set than an actual rain forest. Janet and I are more concerned with bringing a story to life than providing a social studies lesson about West Africa."[2]

Another story with a generalized setting, in both the story text and the illustrations, is Eric Kimmel's *Hershel and the Hanukkah Goblins*. The time and place are in a village in Europe as Hanukkah is about to begin. The illustrations, by Trina Schart Hyman, and the story are an integrated work with story text and illustrations enhancing one another. However, scenes of the village in the illustrations are much more detailed than the setting described in the text of the story.

Yet both *Anansi Goes Fishing* and *Hershel and the Hannukah Goblins* work as all folktales do, so that if readers do not have the illustrations, they can imagine any river shore or village with which they are familiar. Without a specific time, these stories take place long ago, once upon a time.

And, even though the setting may be backdrop, it needs to be accurate and culturally authentic in the story and/or illustrations. Writers, such as Paul Goble, who also illustrate their own books are very aware that both the subject in text and illustrations need to be clear in the representation of cultural aspects of the story.

> Question: "What do you do to make the setting of both the stories and illustrations accurate?"
>
> Paul Goble: "If a myth that I wish to retell has a specific location, and many do, I will, of course, go there to meditate, examine, and get the feel of the place. I note the birds, the flowers, and so on to be included later, perhaps in the illustrations. I go to great lengths to obtain correct information when both writing and illustrating. Nothing is worse in my view than illustrations that are inaccurate or written statements that are untrue. I try very hard not to make such mistakes. I want to *know* what I am drawing. My style doesn't allow for "fudging" or "sketching." I am working with a culture that is like my own. It would be insulting to Indian people to make mistakes. I'm sure I've made some, but I try not to—and Indian people have told me I do a good job."[3]

In "La Llorona," a folktale from old Mexico, a river becomes an important yet undetailed place in the story. A woman disappears, in or near this river, and readers imagine a ghost of this woman—*la llorona*—who appears near the same river. Listeners of these tales create through their imaginations their own river as part of the story. Young writers of tales in the folktale tradition must create settings that show the place to fit the story they wish to tell.

MORE COMPLEX SETTINGS

Some settings might be described in more detail because they are essential to the character and plot development of the story. Stories by individual authors that are written to be read, instead of traditional stories like folktales that were originally written to be heard, have settings that need more detail.

Fictional frameworks in the genres of science fiction, historical fiction, contemporary realistic fiction, and fantasy need detail to make a place come alive, make readers want to be there, and make them want to enter the story and take part in it.

In Allen Say's *Grandfather's Journey*, partially set in Japan prior to, during, and after World War II, the setting is essential and integrated with the characters and plot in such a way that cultural connections are more developed than those of folktales. Likewise, the celebration of Christmas in Japan in Say's *Tree of Cranes* merges or pulls two cultures together—the Christmas tree and a time of rebirth in the Japanese home in a setting where cranes symbolize long life.

USING MEMORIES FROM CHILDHOOD

Young writers need to be aware of the importance of using their own memories in creating place and time. Allen Say, referring to part of the setting in *Tree of Cranes*, makes that importance clear in his comments about his childhood in Japan:

> The big goldfish hatchery next to my old house, where the carp pond in *Tree of Cranes* had been, was now replaced with rows of ugly concrete apartment buildings. The ancient fishing village where my nanny had come from was gone. The fine beach where our maid used to pick seaweed for the evening soup was gone. In fact, the entire seashore had been buried, and a jumble of factories now stood over the playground of my memory. Like Urashima Taro, I had gone back to a world without a past. My childhood was entirely in my mind. A dream.[4]

The sensory images of sight, touch, taste, and smell—images of fish swimming, the touch of seaweed, the taste of soup, the smell of the ocean—are all there in the comments from Allen Say. Young writers need to learn to be perceptive of the world around them and observe—really "see" their worlds and hold them dear in their minds to write about in the stories they create—making places and times real for themselves and making them real for others through their writing.

SETTING THE SCENE

Mildred Taylor, an African American author, uses the "place" of Mississippi where her relatives lived and the Depression times of the 1930s to create setting. In the time in which her stories take place, civil rights for blacks were nonexistent and dramatic scenes of life and death were played out against a rural farming landscape. That setting in such a specific time and place creates a tension, "setting up" scenes in the story to balance the people against the times. Mildred Taylor's fiction, placed in the South in a time of legal segregation, gives readers stories with rural dialect that makes the particular setting in Mississippi realistic. We can see that from the first paragraph and the first scene of *Mississippi Bridge*:

> It was raining and had been all day. Fact, it had been raining for some weeks, a steady, big drop kind of rain that had roads all slopped up outside and ceilings all swollen up and leaking inside. Our ole Mississippi winter it was almost finished, but not quite.[5]

There's a sense of something about to happen, that the weather, which should be changing to spring, is not. The tension inside and outside darkens the beginning of the story. Mildred Taylor gives readers enough detail to understand not just setting, but some connection to the plot. She "foreshadows," or lets readers know that something is going to happen.

LEARNING FROM ADULT LITERATURE

Adult fiction does determine in some ways what happens in fiction for children. Once upon a time the novel had long sections of narrative that contained heavily detailed descriptions of place. Although once a popular part of story construction, long narratives are no longer seen in much contemporary fiction, and stories start more quickly with character and action in both short stories and novels. Brief descriptions of time and place settle the reader into a story almost immediately. For example, *The Fun House*, a short story rewritten as a readers theater for grades 3–8, has time and place (setting) laid out in the beginning two sentences with the characters introduced in the third:

> It was Saturday morning in early spring. The Mosswood Amusement Park had just opened for the season. Shawna and her cousin Edward waited in line for tickets.[6]

HAVING STUDENTS WORK WITH SETTING

To develop young writers' abilities to create more complex settings in their stories, you can choose here from a variety of activities. If students know what and how setting works in stories, they will be able to begin their own writing of sketches or stories.

Journal Activities

Class Journal. In your class, begin a classroom journal in which any student can write. Title the journal "Notes on Setting" for each of the books by Allen Say, Eric Kimmel, Gary Soto, Paul Goble, Mildred Taylor, or other authors of your choice. Students fill in the title and setting for the book that they read. You, as teacher, fill in the ones that you read aloud—making this a collaborative activity.

Individual Journals. Have students close their eyes and listen to the first paragraphs in books such as Eric Kimmel's *Anansi Goes Fishing*, or the first paragraph of chapter 11 from Mildred Taylor's *Roll of Thunder, The Well*, or others. Ask them the following questions, either for discussion or for journal writing:

- What do they see?
- What do they hear?
- What do they feel?

- What could they smell?
- What could they taste?

Reading/Writing/Breaking Setting into Scenes. First, identifying scenes. Like films, stories in print are made up of individual scenes and each scene of the story moves the characters and plot forward. When listening to a story read aloud while watching a film or video from a children's multicultural book, students may note in their journals every time the scene changes and write a few words to show the scene change. On one side of the journal, vertical entries are Scene I, Scene II, Scene III, and so on, while on the other are brief descriptions of the scenes. Then students watch for the switch to the second scene and note that. Younger children may raise their hands when scenes change.

Second, recognizing scene changes. Students count the changes of scene in a story or film and enter that number in their journals after the title. They then compare them with the number that is the correct amount. Questions will arise as to when a change in scene is taking place. Students can discuss how the author tries to make that clear for the reader. Students can also pick a character in a scene and discuss why the scene shows something about the character.

Third, developing the scenery. A story is made up of several scenes that include the place where something happens, the person/character who does something, and some sequence of actions and events. Here is an example to use to show a scene: Michael/Jennifer (or names that students have chosen individually) is a (character). He/she walked to school (place—on the way to school). He/she saw a red bicycle lying near the curb. No one was around. What did he/she do? Ask students to brainstorm ideas for what their character would do next in this scene on the way to school. Then ask students to write a scene with one of the characters listed above.

Vocabulary Connections

On one side of a card, have students write the title of a story and their names. On the other side of the card, have students write words from the story that show setting. These words may become vocabulary words for settings for new stories that students will write. Place cards on large rings so that students can add to them and flip through them to see what words the whole class has compiled.

Assessment: Writing Familiar Settings

Create a large chart with the following label at the top: *Title, Story Setting, What We Know about This Place/Time from Experience*. Fill in the chart with the information. Have students write their own descriptions of places and times for settings that they know. For example, if there is a setting that takes place "near a river," a student who knows what it's like near a river would write a description of the time and place near the river.

Geography: Places That Are Real or Imaginary

Margarita González-Jensen's *The Butterfly Pyramid* takes place near Cancun, Mexico. In that story, the place is real—near a pyramid near Cancun. The scene with the butterflies is imaginary, but could have taken place. By placing the words "butterfly" and "pyramid" in the title, Margarita González-Jensen gives the place "power" and defines what the story is about. Use the following words from Margarita González-Jensen with students:

> There is a connection with nature. Connection with the natural environment, where the coast and jungle come together. The boy gives the old man the seashells. There are the tropical flowers of the jungle. Ice cream in tropical flavors, like lemon, mamey, tamarind, and coconut—the kinds I would have eaten in Cancun.[7]

After reading stories in which actual locations are given, have a large map of the world in the classroom on which the place of stories can be marked to show that authors write about different places that reflect global and multicultural perspectives.

For places that do not exist in fact, such as Terabithia, from Katherine Paterson's *Bridge to Terabithia*, place markers as near as possible to a place that is real if there is one identified in the story, or create new maps of "imaginary places." Students can also mark on the map the real or imaginary places from their own stories.

Maps of Paths in Stories

Students may draw maps to show the path a character takes or follows and what it is like.

They can create general time lines to show the passage of time and what the main character does and when he or she does it.

Finding Descriptors through Paired Writing

Using the same story, two students work together to find time and place in a story. Focus questions that may be on paper or on the computer include:

- When and where does the story take place?
- What words in the story make that clear for you?
- Is the setting one you have experienced?
- Where and when were you in this setting or one like it?
- How important is setting to understanding character?

Compare and Contrast Places Called "Home"

In small groups, have students compare the homes in *Tree of Cranes* in Japan with the home in Gary Soto's *Too Many Tamales* or other picture storybooks or novels students have read. Use Venn diagrams with overlap for similarities. Ask students to write their own conclusions about similarities and differences.

Travel Brochures

Students may design a travel brochure for the setting of a book that you have read aloud or they have read on their own. Students create at least one paragraph with details of setting. They use sense imagery (what they feel, see, hear, smell, and taste). By using details to make the setting specific, they can try and convince people that they would like to travel there. To express "mood," they can use words that create "places" of excitement or thrills, relaxation or comfort, or a place where they can learn and be involved with the place and people/animals/characters there.

Fantasy: Place of Dreams

Use Allen Say's *Stranger in the Mirror*, *River Dream* for lower grades, or *The Sign Painter* and Lawrence Yep's *Tree of Dreams: Ten Tales from the Garden of Night* for upper grades. In a discussion, ask students what is fantasy (or dreamlike) and what is real in the story used.

Have students write a story in which a young boy or girl imagines himself or herself somewhere else, going through events and then back home. In the writing, students need to include the five senses to make their fantasies realistic.

Places: Created by People or Natural Surroundings

Students have places in their lives that are either made by people or are natural landscapes. Some of the places are included here with authors, and multicultural books that focus on those kinds of settings. Using multicultural books from the lists below or from choices of your own, complete the following activity with students. In small groups, have students:

- Describe the place they know about from their experience.
- Describe the place of the story read from the text (print).
- Describe the place of the story from the illustrations only.

Places Made by People

Libraries: Curtis, Christopher Paul. *Bud, Not Buddy*; Kimmel, Eric. *I Took My Frog to the Library*

Ask students to write a short piece on what their library looks like or what their "perfect imaginary" library would look like. Who would they see there or who or what would they take with them to the library?

Sports and Ballparks: Bruchac, Joseph. *Children of the Longhouse* (historic fiction—lacrosse ball games); Myers, Walter Dean. *Mop, Moondance, and the Nagasaki Knights*; Myers, Walter Dean. *Me, Mop, and the Moondance Kid*; Say, Allen. *El Chino*; Yep, Laurence. *Sea Glass*

Ask students to compare their sports places with those from these stories. Have students write short descriptions of places where sports take place. What would they see, hear, smell, feel, and taste there?

Schools: Ada, Alma Flor. *My Name Is María Isabel*; Allen Say. *Allison*; Allen Say. *Emma's Rug*; Choi, Nyul Sook. *Halmoni and the Picnic*; Hamilton, Virginia. *The Planet of Junior Brown*; Hoffman, Mary. *Amazing Grace*; Littlesugar, Amy. *Freedom School, Yes!*; Woodson, Jacqueline. *Maizon at Blue Hill*; Yep, Laurence. *Thief of Hearts*

Ask students to describe what their school looks like. What do they hear, smell, taste, and feel there?

Cities: Myers, Walter Dean. *Won't Know Until I Get There*; Orlev, Uri. *The Island on Bird Street*; Soto, Gary. *Chato's Kitchen*; Yep, Laurence. *The Case of the Goblin Pearls*; Yep, Laurence. *The Cook's Family*

Have students write responses to the following: On their way to school, what do students see, hear, smell, feel, and taste? What character could they come up with who could live in a city? In the country?

Cemeteries and Graveyards: Tate, Eleanora E. *The Secret of Gumbo Grove*

Ask students about their experiences with cemeteries or graveyards and what they would see or hear there.

Places That Are Natural

Like many authors, Allen Say is very much aware of the natural world.

Question by Martha Davis Beck: "The natural landscape seems important to you. Were you tuned in to your surroundings as a child?"

Allen Say: "I have moved so many times in my life that each time—I've done this since I was a kid—I've tried to memorize the place, thinking that it might be the last time that I'm going to see that scene. . . . What's happening now is that the American landscape has finally entered my bloodstream. I'm working on it right now in a book called *The Sign Painter*. It's my tribute to the land, and a comment on what we're doing to it."[8]

Forests and Jungles: Ho, Minfong. *The Clay Marble*; Kimmel, Eric. *Anansi and the Moss-Covered Rock* (illustrations are like a stage setting); Paterson, Katherine. *The Tale of the Mandarin Ducks*; Salisbury, Graham. *Jungle Dogs*

Deserts and Plains: Bruchac, Joseph. *Between Earth and Sky: Legends of Native American Sacred Places* (deserts, mountains, plains, forests); Cohen, Caron Lee. *The Mud Pony: A Traditional Skidi Pawnee Tale* (Illustrated by Shonto Begay); Duncan, Lois. *The Magic of Spider Woman* (Illustrated by Shonto Begay); Say, Allen. *The Sign Painter*

Sea: Kimmel, Eric. *Billy Lazroe and the King of the Sea*; Martin, Rafe. *The Shark God*; Yep, Laurence. *Sea Glass*; Yep, Laurence. *The Dragon Prince: A Chinese Beauty and the Beast Tale*

Sharpening Observational Skills and Ideas for Writing

Using Sight. While students are sitting in the classroom, ask them to write down words for those things that they *see* around them. Print those words on large sheets of paper to hang around the room. Then make other lists of the things that you see that make sounds, things that you see that you can touch, things you can see that you smell. Post the lists. Students may use those lists for ideas, increasing their use of the senses in the development of scenes in stories.

Sound and Setting in Stories. Using books either read aloud or that students have read on their own, have students figure out the sounds that are in the story or could be in the story. Then have them create the sounds, perhaps with music, and tape them to fit the story read aloud. Students can write their own scene descriptions with the same sounds.

On Time

In a discussion, using an overhead projector, a large sheet of paper, or a chalkboard, ask students to compare the beginning of the school day in a story among those listed earlier in the chapter with the beginning of a school day in your classroom. Use connecting circles with overlap for those things that are similar. Ask the following questions:

- What things are the same?
- What things are different?
- How are they different?
- What would you taste, touch, feel, see, and hear in the morning?
- What would you taste, touch, feel, see, and hear in the afternoon?

Weather in a Story

Draw a circle on the board and tell students to imagine that they are at the beach/seashore. Use variations of the following statements: Imagine this place when it is sunny. What could you as a character see hear, taste, smell, feel? Now imagine a different kind of weather where the beach/seashore is dark and stormy. What would your character see, hear, taste, smell, and feel? Some stories with storms to use are Mildred Taylor's *Roll of Thunder, Hear My Cry*; Paul Goble's *The Girl Who Loved Wild Horses, The Legend of the White Buffalo Woman*, or *Iktomi and the Boulder*; Eric Kimmel's *Billy Lazroe and the King of the Sea*; Patricia Polacco's *Thundercake*; Virginia Hamilton's *Drylongso*; or Virginia Driving Hawk Sneve's *Jimmy Yellow Hawk*.

Seasons in a Story

Using a story listed below with one of the seasons, ask students to describe what it is like, using words that show the senses: see, hear, smell, taste, touch.

Winter: Bruchac, Joseph. *The Boy Who Lived with the Bears and Other Iroquois Stories*; Curtis, Christopher Paul. *Bud, Not Buddy*; Kimmel, Eric. *Sirko and the Wolf*; Kimmel, Eric. *Hershel and the Hanukkah Goblins*; Medearis, Angela Shelf. *Poppa's Itchy Christmas*; Orlev, Uri. *Island on Bird Street*; Polacco, Patricia. *The Trees of the Dancing Goats*; Say, Allen. *Tree of Cranes*; Yep, Laurence. *Dream Soul*

Winter/Spring and Spring/Fall: Kimmel, Eric. *Billy Lazroe and the King of the Sea*; Kimmel, Eric. *The Bird's Gift: A Ukranian Easter Story*

Summer: Bruchac, Joseph. *The First Strawberries*; Goble, Paul. *Star Boy*; Medearis, Angela Shelf. *Dancing with the Indians*; Myers, Walter Dean. *Won't Know Until I Get There*; Soto, Gary. *Summer on Wheels*

Fall: Goble, Paul. *Love Flute*

All Seasons: Bruchac, Joseph. *Fox Song*; Bruchac, Joseph. *Thirteen Moons on Turtle's Back*; Bruchac, Joseph. *A Boy Called Slow*

Understanding How Time Works/Creating Time Lines for a Story

Using a work of children's literature such as *Anansi Goes Fishing* for younger grades or Uri Orlev's *Island on Bird Street* for older students, have students write words to show the passage of time in a story. Then with students, create a time line, either in written or pictorial form, for the setting of the story. This pictorial time line is a storyboard based on setting of a story. (Most storyboards are done for the action or plot of the story.)

In small groups, students can go over their time lines. If the story takes place in a day, with times listed, a clock could be used instead of a time line to show the time changes. Seasons can be shown by four blocks on paper. Months can be used with blank calendars that students fill in with what things happened to their characters during those months. Questions students should answer are: Which event follows which? and What is the setting like for each event?

Historical Fiction and Settings

With historical fiction, setting is an integral part of the plot because the details are necessary for a sense of history. Read the first four pages of the historical fiction by Mildred Taylor, Katherine Paterson, Christopher Paul Curtis, or another historical fiction author, and discuss the time and place of each. Focus questions:

- Where does the action take place?
- What are the connections of characters in a time and place?
- How is what happens in the story linked to the time and place?
- Why does the author of these stories have to show you time and place in more detail?

Writing Historical Time and Place Descriptions

Have students write a brief description of a time and place of their choice, focusing on details that show a particular time and place. Some sample story beginnings to use for historical settings might include: "It is in 700 A.D., the 1850s, or 1950s, and so on, in (place). Students may use social studies texts, library references, or the Internet for ideas to give a sense of place and time in history."

Setting in Historic Fiction Compared with the Present and Future

After reading from Mildred Taylor's *Roll of Thunder, Hear My Cry* or Laurence Yep's *Dragonwings*, have students compare the time frame of then and now.

Discussion Activity. Ask students the following questions:

- What things do people have that are the same today as when the story took place?
- What things do people have that are different now compared with then?
- Why do we have things that are different today?

Writing Activity. Ask students to write two paragraphs: one that shows a character with possessions from a time long ago and one that shows a character with possessions from today. As a variation: Future Time for Science Fiction or Fantasy. Complete the same activity using the present and the future instead of the past and the present. Use the following discussion questions:

- What things do people have today?
- What things will people have in the future that are the same as today?
- What things will people have in the future that will be different from today?

Rewriting Endings

Read a variant of a folktale and have students rewrite the story using a different ending, making sure that they have time and place and weather in the story.

Assessment: Conventions of Folktales

Place is familiar as "long, long ago" or "once upon a time" in the folktales of some cultures. Students can use that way to begin stories.

At the end of their stories, they can use the line "They lived happily ever after." Students may use a cultural variation for beginnings and endings of stories from their own backgrounds. For example, many Middle Eastern tales begin, "Once there was, once there was not."

Ask students to write a folktale modeled on one that they have read. Have them decide what will happen in the beginning and the end to show setting and cause and effect.

CHAPTER 4

What: Plot in a Story

Coming up with characters—at least names and gender—is not a daunting task for students, but coming up with detailed characterization for their characters is. It is important to have students spend time developing their characters. After they decide on the main characters for a story and they can describe what those characters are like, they need to figure out what happens to their characters in a story. By understanding what their characters need and want (the problem in the story), students can create a plot with a conflict. That conflict has the character in opposition to an antagonist (a character or adverse circumstance) that tries to keep the main character from getting what he or she needs or wants or from reaching his or her goal.

To further their understanding of plot, young writers need to work with plots from the literature written for them. Literacy classroom activities, such as making predictions, story retellings, or plot reconstruction (changing story elements), can help writers understand characters and their relation to plot—the problem or struggle for solution in a chronology of events that lead to climax and resolution. A sequence of story events, placed in a chart or on a graph, can give you and young writers a way to lay out plot structures in stories.

STORY SEQUENCE WITH CHARACTER

Walter Dean Myers advises young writers about the importance of understanding that a question or problem can help determine the plot of a story:

By turning every idea into a clear question or problem the story or essay becomes infinitely easier to write. In fiction the problem must be of essential importance to the central characters. The "solution" to the problem then becomes the plot. In essays or nonfiction, the question gives a logical direction to the essay. This technique, carefully considered in the prewriting stage, should make writing easier.[1]

A fictional character tries to solve a problem of "essential importance." But how do writers come up with the characters and their problems or the plot of the story?

Joseph Bruchac tells us that sometimes an author's own experiences or feelings determine the "story." Other times, the plots may come from historical events, incidents, or the oral tradition of storytelling:

> I can't say that any of the events in my childhood have turned into the plot for any other writing than autobiographical—with the possible exception of *Fox Song*. However, things that some of my characters feel about themselves are much influenced by my memories of how I felt when I was that same age. When Chris Nicola in *The Heart of a Chief* arrives at school for his first day of sixth grade, his feelings and some of the things that happen to him mirror my own experiences. And Young Hunter, in my novel for young adults *Dawn Land*, is my alter ego in a few places, even though that novel takes place thousands of years ago. More often than not, though, I draw plot from histories quite apart from my own experience—as in *Arrow over the Door* (an incident from the American Revolution) or *Sacajawea* (the journey of Lewis and Clark)— or from oral traditions, building my fiction around the plots of traditional stories, as in *Dawn Land*. I also listen to the stories that kids tell me and they sometimes become part of my plots—as in the cases of both *Eagle Song* and *The Heart of a Chief*, which I owe a great deal to a number of Native kids who described to me their experiences in non-Native schools.[2]

Writers may start with characters and then determine their plot in detail, or they may choose to start with plot as they write their stories. If authors think of some conflict, such as a relationship or some sort of event, and then develop characters to engage in that conflict, they are thinking of plot rather than character to begin their story. Because no hard-and-fast rules exist for determining whether to begin with character or plot, young writers need to decide for themselves whether character or plot is more important in the initial development of a particular story.

It does seem, however, that starting with character gives young writers something to "hold on to" as they develop ideas for problems and solutions for stories. Working with students, you can use various multicultural authors from this book and others to show how ideas turn into plots for stories.

Virginia Driving Hawk Sneve talks about her ideas for the plot of *The Chichi HooHoo Bogeyman* as well the beginnings of "characters" for her story.

> Question: "How did you come up with the plot for *The Chichi Hoohoo Bogeyman?*"
>
> Virginia Driving Hawk Sneve: "In the town of Flandreau, South Dakota, where we had lived, there was a middle-aged Indian man who was deaf-mute. Children often teased him, and he would pretend to chase them to drive them away—his experiences gave me the idea for the plot."[3]

In *High Elk's Treasure*, she also uses connections to her Sioux background—"an event"—for the beginning of a plot:

> "I was doing research for a nonfiction project and found the '100 years' agreement' among warriors who fought at Little Big Horn—not to reveal who killed Custer until a century had passed. They were afraid of retribution by the U.S. government. The knowledge supposedly orally passed through generations. Also there was a horse, Comanche, which survived the battle even though he had been wounded."[4]

Virginia Driving Hawk Sneve's *Jimmy Yellow Hawk* can also be used to show a simple and effective plot structure with the title character. The main character is upset because he is called "Little Jim" while his father is "Big Jim" (problem). He wants and needs to be viewed by his friends and family as more grown up instead of as a little kid. He is tired of being teased by the other boys (character revealed). That need for being seen as more grown up, resulting in his desire for a new name, results in conflicts within himself as he seeks a new name by trying to do something "brave." He changes and grows as he faces different obstacles, and in the end he becomes "Jimmy Yellow Hawk," a ten-year-old with a nickname of his own, instead of being called the diminutive of "Little Jim" (resolution).[5]

A picture storybook to compare with *Jimmy Yellow Hawk* is the story of Sitting Bull, *A Boy Called Slow*, written by Joseph Bruchac. This story also focuses on the importance of a name in the Sioux tribe. It wouldn't be too hard for young writers to see the conflict inside and outside a character in the "calling" of a name in either of these stories.

FASTER ENTRANCE INTO THE STORY LINE

Actions do speak louder than words. And what has changed in fiction writing in the last half century is that the action starts on the first page, with little description or narrative. Background information about characters might appear later in the story. Long descriptive passages of a character no longer dominate literature. Rather, character descriptions may occur later in the story as summary in the narrative so that the action is not slowed or stopped.

NARRATIVE ORDER OF THE PLOT

The narrative order of a plot in most stories is usually chronological, with events that take place in sequence from the past to the present and future. Sometimes, however, the narrative may include *flashbacks* or *foreshadowing*.

Flashbacks are scenes that take place in the past of the story. They are not remembrances of what took place in the past, but scenes that the writer actually places in the past after he or she has set the main story in the present. The writer begins in the present or future, then goes back to the past, and then comes forward. In books, such as novels, writers need to get a reader's attention early in the story and begin with present action, then go to the past to "flashback" to an earlier story (time and place) to explain what is happening right now.

Flashback is not a literary technique that appears often in literature for younger readers because younger children do not have a well-developed sense of time. It is difficult for them to be able to be in a present time and place, make a transition to earlier times, and then make a transition to present and future.

Stories for younger readers therefore operate on a chronological plot line without flashbacks. They begin at one point and go from start to finish. *Anansi Goes Fishing*, *Allison*, and *The Gold Coin* are examples of chronological plot stories.

Foreshadowing may occur in any story. This technique works to hint, through clues given to the reader, at what will happen in the next scene or chapter. These clues may occur via a character's words, thoughts, or actions, or scene description. Foreshadowing clues may set a mood for a story to pull us in or may happen within the story to make us want to turn the page to see what happens next. The opening paragraph of *Hershel and the Hannukah Goblins* hints at what will happen next, in a very clear and concise manner for readers:

> It was the first night of Hanukkah. Hershel of Ostropol was walking down the road. He was tired and hungry. Nonetheless, his step was light. Soon he would reach the next village, where bright candles, merry songs, and platters piled high with tasty potato latkes awaited him.
>
> But when he arrived, the village was silent and dark. Not a single Hanukkah candle could be seen.[6]

It's easy to see that things are not right in the village and that something has happened so that Hanukkah is not taking place. Also, if you have young writers look closely at the illustrations in *Hershel and the Hanukkah Goblins* as well as at the text, you can help students see how foreshadowing also appears in the illustrations. Other multicultural picture storybooks will also be fine sources for viewing foreshadowing— integrated in both text and illustrations.

However, advanced techniques, such as going back to the past for more "story" in terms of long flashbacks or hinting at future action with extensive foreshadowing, are more appropriate for upper elementary student writers with a better developed sense of time to use in their writing.

TWO KINDS OF PLOT STRUCTURES

The knowledge of the chronological narrative order gives writers the ability to convey events and scenes from earlier to later time. Within that chronological framework, plots may be *progressive* or *episodic*. Most picture storybooks, chapter books, and novels are progressive—a story begins, a character (or characters) has a problem and goes through events, the story reaches a climax, and finally the story reaches a resolution. Characters along the way struggle as they engage in the conflicts around a central problem. That conflict/tension/struggle moves toward resolution and the wrapping up of the story. The author or writer usually ties everything together in the end.

Gary Soto's *Too Many Tamales* is a progressive plot structure where a young girl loses her mother's wedding ring while making tamales for the holiday season. That plot line, the struggle by the main character to make things right and solve the "problem" in the story, resolves the plot of the story.

Another example is the plot of *Allison* by Allen Say, a Japanese author and illustrator. A young girl finds out that she is adopted and that her birth parents have given her up. As she tries to come to terms with this fact, she finds a stray cat. In taking the cat in (even though Allen Say doesn't tell us explicitly), Allison is coming to terms with her identity and adoption, resolving her problem.

Episodic plot structures have the same main characters in many of the chapters, but the stories read as "episodes," or short stories, with the story held together by the characters who are in the stories. Mary Hoffman's *Starring Grace* is a chapter book that is primarily episodic but does have a minimal central plot. Gary Soto's *Baseball in April and Other Stories* also has an episodic structure since the stories are linked by some of the same main characters, but each chapter is a separate short story with a character solving a problem within it. Gary Soto uses events from his childhood as plots or events in his fictional stories:

> The title story *Baseball in April* is based loosely on my own experience of waiting for the little league coach to call and say, "You're in." Other than this one story, however, all my work is the stuff of the imagination, or stuff that I hear from others. One case in point is "The Squirrels" from *Local News*. That story is based loosely on a conversation with my wife's pastor, Alpha Gato. Another case in point is "Barbie," a story of a doll who loses her head. I heard this story somewhere along the line and saved it until I was prepared to set it down onto the page.[7]

In any plot structure, characters need something. Somehow in the story, they try to figure out how to get their needs or wants met—solving problems. Also, characters have to have the kind of traits or characterization that would make them able to solve problems. As young writers develop plots, a lot of "what ifs" can help them figure out their characters and structure their plot lines. Following are some questions students could ask themselves:

- What if my character is poor and wants to be wealthy?
- What if my character is wealthy and becomes poor?
- What if my character is trying to take advantage of another character and the tables turn?
- What flaw does my character have that doesn't allow him or her to get what he or she wants?
- Is my character greedy? Is my character brave?
- What makes my character change in the story?

In Eric Kimmel's African story *Anansi Goes Fishing*, Anansi, the main character, has a flaw. He thinks he is so smart and sees himself as the perfect trickster. But his belief in his ability to trick the other animals leads to his downfall in this story when he is outwitted.

In other fictional stories, characters may have flaws that cause problems that somehow must be resolved in the story. In other words, they make mistakes. They don't always make the right decisions or take the right actions, but readers believe in them and go with them as they change and grow in a story. Any flaws that they have make them all the more interesting to readers. It's important for writers to know that their characters can be imperfect as they work on their own new stories. Below are two variations of charts that you can use with students to lay out story structures in stories read or in stories that students are writing or have written:

Story Sequence with Plot Focus
Character: Wants or needs something
Setting: When? Where?
Plot: Someone or something keeps the character from getting what he or she needs or wants. What happens?

Story Sequence with Character Focus

Main character is opposed by what? Then does what? Because . . . does/goes/sees.

Main character then does what because. . . . Then does what because. . . .

Main character solves his or her problem by doing what?

Characters and plots together make a story worth reading. The character is one who acts to solve a problem, and the plot is where the struggle/problem/action takes place. And that struggle takes place in a three-stage process with a beginning, a middle, and an end. Each action (or insight) that involves a character has a cause and an effect. The "structuring of plot" includes thinking about cause-and-effect relationships. And, in the fictional worlds writers create, aspects of plot must be tied down, with few loose ends.

THE POINT OF VIEW OF THE READER

A reader is very aware of cause and effect in stories. In Eric Kimmel's *Anansi Goes Fishing*, the *cause* of Anansi's problems is his wish to trick the turtle, another animal in the story. The *results* of the action of the story are a "turnabout" in that Anansi is tricked himself. The whole story gives readers the satisfaction of having understood why things were the way they were in the first place. Readers identify with a character. They "shadow" or become that character as they read and go through the scenes in the story and engage in problems, struggles, and the story's resolution.

THE POINT OF VIEW OF THE WRITER

The characters, held in their places by plot structure, are moved forward by the writer, who determines what causes and what effects will take place.

CONFLICT IN STORY

In order for a story to have cause and effect, actions take place that involve some sort of conflict with a main character (protagonist). That conflict in plot development may be any of the following or some of the following combined:

- person against person
- person against self
- person against nature
- person against some part of society

The conflicts of "person against" are included, with book titles, in the activity section. Regardless of what the conflict is, the main character has some problem to solve and someone or something is keeping that from happening.

Why Is It Hard to Develop Conflict in Stories?

Conflict is one of the hardest areas for any writer to work with because conflict goes against peace, tranquillity, stasis, and serenity—the kind of atmosphere we want around ourselves in our real world. Yet young writers have to think about conflict, imagine characters in conflict, and create conflict that is believable.

You can easily show students how problems and resolutions, or causes and effects, involve some conflict by having students look at plots of traditional literature, such as folktales. In these stories, character is not as important as plot. Told in the oral tradition, which values one-dimensional characters who are easily identified, such as the wicked king or queen, the strong woman or man, the foolish husband or wife, these stories are easy to take apart to see how they work.

With simple settings, these stories don't require much description on the part of student writers. It could be a dark forest or a small village, or something similar. Readers' imaginations create their own forests or villages. Let's suppose that it is night. You and your students are sitting near a campfire. A storyteller stands before you. "Once upon a time," she begins. She tells you a story about a man so upset with the noise of his wife and children in such a small house (problem) that he can't live one more day in that house (conflict). He seeks help from a wise person in the village, the Rabbi, who gives him advice. The man takes the advice of the Rabbi. Over and over again, the man complains and the Rabbi on each visit tells him to move more and more of his animals into his house. Of course, the noise level is overwhelming. The conflict remains and worsens, but then when he goes back to the Rabbi, the Rabbi says to remove all of the animals in the house (solution/resolution). The house, noisy, then noisier with all the animals, seems quieter. That shortened variant is an old Yiddish tale. It contains the elements of plot construction.

In folktales, with the plots taking precedence over characters, each character's wants and needs are subservient to what is happening in the story. Sometimes a tale may contain a message for children. In *La Llorona*, "The Weeper," and other variants of this Mexican tale, there is a main character, a woman who weeps eternally for her lost children. This "ghost" entices children or others lost, along the river, on empty streets, or near dark woods, to come with her. And the message of parents, after telling this tale to their children, includes a warning: "Stay away from the river—or the streets—or the woods. *La llorona* might get you." Or perhaps they might say, "Strange cries at night have been heard along the river. Watch out. It's *la llorona*."

Folktales from various cultures are story forms that young writers can use to construct simple plots, and they can use their own cultural backgrounds to create the characters and names for the characters. Characters in their Hispanic tales could have Hispanic names, in Italian tales the characters could have Italian names, in African tales they could have African names, and so on. Settings and plots may occur in countries that reflect the cultural backgrounds of young writers.

HOW DO WRITERS FIGURE OUT PLOTS?

Writers of children's literature get their ideas for plot structures from many sources, including, as Walter Dean Myers does, connecting original thoughts in such a way as to come up with very creative stories.

Question: "How did you come up with the plot for *The Blues of Flats Brown*?"

Walter Dean Myers: "In *The Blues of Flats Brown* I wondered if the same mistreatment that made a junk yard dog mean might also be the inspiration for artistic statement, i.e., the Blues. The idea of having him travel gave me the chance to bring different cities, settings, and travel into the story, which are typical of the blues genre."[8]

But how will your young writers decide what will happen in a story? As talked about earlier in this chapter, any plot has a problem and a resolution. Most students understand what "a problem" is. By referring to story problems from mathematics and using the term "solution," you can assist students' understanding of the term "resolution." Also, by having students examine plot structures from books read to them or by them, you can facilitate their movement to the creation of their own plots. The following plot activities expand on the understanding of plot structures by giving young writers practice in identifying plot construction and creating plots of their own.

Journal Activity

After all students have read the same story, pair students together to discuss and write in their journals the following: the title of the story and two events (things that happen in the story). Each student chooses one or the other of the two events from the journal entry and writes one of the events on a large card. On another card, each student draws a picture to show the event. Display the cards one above another in story sequence as an ongoing chart or bulletin board.

Assessment: Identifying Plot from a Story

After having read or listened to a multicultural book read aloud, students write the title of the story down the left side of the paper and a sentence next to the letters of the title to show what happens in the story. For younger children, you may complete a chart with children in a group and then post the chart with created sentences in the room.

Beginning, Middle, and End:
Using Visuals with Reading and Writing

Webbing the Plot. Using a book read to students or one that they read themselves, write the title in the middle of a sheet of paper and draw three lines extending from it with the labels *beginning*, *middle*, and *end* below each. Students may write words or sentences under each category to show the three main parts of a story.

Drawing the Plot. Divide a paper vertically in thirds with the title above and each third labeled as *beginning*, *middle*, and *end*. Students then write sentences and illustrate one event that occurs in the three main parts of a story. They may discuss their story layouts in small groups and place them up for display, or scan them for computer use, filed under particular stories for future use by you or other students.

Reader Response Connections

Tying children's responses to plots of stories is a way to allow children to understand and construct plots. Ask students the following question for any of the books mentioned earlier in this chapter: What happened to (a character) in (story)? Then, from their own direct experiences, students can answer the following questions:

- Has anything like that ever happened to you?
- What did you do to get through it?
- Was there a time when you had a problem?
- What kept you from solving the problem?
- What did you do? How?

Sparking ideas for plot construction can lead to the creation of a variety of plots.

Vertical Story Layout

Using a multicultural book of your choice, have students lay out the story in vertical format on paper, beginning with the following placed in a vertical line:

Title
Characters
Problem
Events leading to resolution
Resolution

Students can work in pairs, in groups, in pairs on computers, or in small groups to complete this activity on plot knowledge. They may place their responses to each part of the story layout next to the appropriate category.

Comparing Plot Structures

Use two versions of the same story, such as Alma Flor Ada's *The Rooster Who Went to His Uncle's Wedding* and Lucia M. González' *The Bossy Gallito* (illustrated by Lulu Delacre). Students can compare and contrast the literary elements of the story, such as character, setting, and plot, and then write their own version of the same story.

Characters need to have at least one trait that defines who they are, no matter if they are in the simplest folktale or most complicated novel. For example, the rooster from *The Rooster Who Went to His Uncle's Wedding* has to be clean and on time. He is extremely persistent in being so. But that need to be clean also means that he is too proud of how he looks and because of that pride almost does not make it to his uncle's wedding on time.

As a variation, have students change the animal to one of their choice and write the same story with this different character.

Retelling in Writing

After students have read, or you have read aloud, a multicultural story, give students the following statement: Imagine you are a TV reporter from (setting of the story). Retell what happens in the story in your own words. Write a sentence that answers each of the following questions:

- Who is the main character in the story?
- What did this character do?
- What happened?
- Where did it happen?
- When did it happen?
- Why did it happen?

Students should have at least six sentences when they finish.

Focus on Character, Identification of Problem, and Conflict

This activity demonstrates how conflict in plot structure moves characters forward who continue to act until some solution is reached. Following are some questions to ask students:

- What is the main character's problem?
- What were the things that happened to keep the main character from solving his or her problem?
- What did the character do to keep trying to solve the problem?
- What was the most exciting event in the story?
- What was the solution to the problem?
- When and where was the problem/conflict solved/resolved?
- How was it solved/resolved?

Assessment: Plot Comparison of Conflicts

Main plot structures are basically the following: *person against person*, *person against self*, *person against the environment/nature*, and *person against society*. The word *against* means that there is a conflict in which the main character must make choices. Those choices will result in either some accomplishment, some success gained, or some decision that the character makes as a result of the problems that he or she faces going through the story events.

Have students compare the plots of stories with two person-against-person conflicts, two person-against-self conflicts, two person-against-nature conflicts, or two person-against-society conflicts by listing what is the same and what is different about the conflicts in the stories. After they have completed their lists, they can work in groups to come up with a plot for the type of conflict that they have reviewed in the books and share that with the whole class.

Developing Person-Against-Person Conflicts into a Short Story. Use the following statement to help students get started: "Imagine that your character has a problem that involves another character." Suggested book titles for person-against-person plot structures are listed below. For grades K–3:

Bruchac, Joseph. *The First Strawberries: A Cherokee Story*.
Kimmel, Eric. *Anansi Goes Fishing* or another "Anansi" story.
Lester, Julius. *Sam and the Tigers: A New Telling of* Little Black Sambo.
Myers, Walter Dean. *How Mr. Monkey Saw the Whole World*.
Myers, Walter Dean. *Mr. Monkey and the Gotcha Bird*.
Young, Ed. *The Terrible Nung Gwama*.
Young, Ed. *Lon Po Po: A Red-Riding Hood Story from China*.

For grades 4 and up:

Kimmel, Eric. *Bernal & Florinda: A Spanish Tale*.
Kimmel, Eric. *Billy Lazroe and the King of the Sea*.
Myers, Walter Dean. *Won't Know Until I Get There*.
Salisbury, Graham. *Jungle Dogs*.
Sneve, Virginia Driving Hawk. *Betrayed*.
Sneve, Virginia Driving Hawk. *The Chichi Hoohoo Bogeyman*.
Yep, Laurence. *Cockroach Cooties*.
Yep, Laurence. *Ribbons*.

Developing Person-Against-Self Conflicts into a Short Story. Use the following statement to help students get started: "Imagine that your character has a problem inside, for instance fear, anger, or facing a loss, that he or she must work out." Following is a list of books that have a person struggling with something inside/against himself or herself. For grades K–3:

Ada, Alma Flor. *My Name Is María Isabel*.
Say, Allen. *Allison*.

For grades 4 and up:

Curtis, Christopher Paul. *Bud, Not Buddy*.
Sneve, Virginia Driving Hawk. *Jimmy Yellow Hawk*.

Developing Person-Against-the-Environment/Nature Conflicts into a Short Story. Use the following statement to help students get

started: "Imagine that your character has a problem that involves surviving a natural event like a fire, a flood, or a storm. Where? When?
Why?" Following is a list of books to use that have examples of
person-against-environment/nature. For grades K–3:

Goble, Paul. *The Girl Who Loved Wild Horses.*
Goble, Paul. *Iktomi and the Boulder.*

For grades 4 and up:

Bruchac, Joseph. *Flying with the Eagle, Racing the Great Bear: Sto-
ries from Native North America.*
Myers, Walter Dean. *Shadow of the Red Moon* (middle school to
young adult).
Sneve, Virginia Driving Hawk. *High Elk's Treasure.*
Taylor, Mildred D. *The Mississippi Bridge.*

Developing Person-Against-Society Conflicts into a Short Story.
Use the following statement to help students get started: "Imagine that
the character in your story has a problem with rules in society or fitting
in, or faces a moral dilemma." Following are possible book choices
demonstrating person-against-society conflicts. For grades K–3:

Ada, Alma Flor. *My Name is María Isabel.*
Polacco, Patricia. *The Butterfly.*
Uchida, Yoshiko. *The Bracelet.*

For grades 4 and up:

Choi, Sook Nyul. *The Year of Impossible Goodbyes.*
Curtis, Christopher Paul. *The Watsons Go to Birmingham—1963.*
McKissack, Patricia. *Run Away Home.*
Myers, Walter Dean. *Me, Mop, and the Moondance Kid.*
Salisbury, Graham. *Under the Blood-Red Sun.*
Sneve, Virginia Driving Hawk. *When Thunders Spoke.*
Taylor, Mildred D. *The Gold Cadillac.*
Taylor, Mildred D. *Mississippi Bridge.*

Taylor, Mildred D. *The Friendship.*
Uchida, Yoshiko. *Journey to Topaz.*
Uchida, Yoshiko. *Journey Home.*
Yep, Laurence. *Child of the Owl.*

Listening, Writing, and Mapping

Students listen to a story read aloud. They then write their own versions of the story and read them aloud in small groups. They create their own story maps for their stories and compare their own story maps in small groups.

Comparisons of the Events in Variants of the Same Folktales

Read. Read several variants of *Cinderella* or another folktale and group students for discussion. Ask them to discuss the events that make up the plot of different versions of the story. Each student then writes a list of the events in one of the variants of the story read. Students compare the list of events for different versions of the same tale in small groups. Following are some focus questions for the groups:

- How are the plots the same?
- How they are different?
- What are the different cultural connections for each?

The following list offers some variations on the Cinderella story:

Hayes, Joe. *Little Gold Star/Estrellita de oro. A Cinderella Story.*
Hickox, Rebecca. *The Golden Sandal: A Middle Eastern Cinderella Story* (Middle Eastern).
Martin, Rafe. *The Rough-Face Girl* (Native American: Algonquin).
Steptoe, John. *Mufaro's Beautiful Daughters* (African tale, from the area that is now Zimbabwe).
Young, Ed. *Yeh Shen* (Chinese tale).

Write. After reading two variations of the same tale, such as *The Legend of the White Buffalo Woman* by Paul Goble and the *White*

Buffalo Calf Woman by Joseph Bruchac, have students write their own version of the white buffalo calf woman legend.

Compare. Using Shonto Begay's *Ma'ii and Cousin Horned Toad* and Eric Kimmel's *Anansi Goes Fishing*, ask students to compare the tales. Ask the following question: What is the same and what is different about the plots of these two stories? Students can write their answers on cards, or you can work with a larger group on an overhead projector or computer to keep track of similarities and differences.

Use Plot Construction and Illustration. After comparing the plot structures of the above or two other similar books, have students choose one of the books and write one sentence on a 3 × 5 card to show how one illustration moves the plot along.

Story Event Posters

Have students create a poster that shows a scene from one of Gary Soto's or another writer's books. Students write on the poster what story event is happening in the scene that they choose to display. Include the title and author on the poster. Have students explain their posters to the class. Line up the posters around the room to show the sequence of the story and story events.

From Story Summary to Poetry

Students write the summary of the plot of any story in one paragraph. Then from this summary they can create a modified *cinquain*, a five-line poem that follows the form of two words in the first line, four words in the second line, six words in the third line, eight words in the fourth line, and two words in the final line. The title of the story may be the title of the poem.

With younger primary students, create the poem as a language experience chart. With intermediate students, create a template that has the numbers on the left with lines for them to write the words on the right.

Writing about Characters on Journeys

Students can write a story about a character whom they describe and who goes on a trip and encounters problems on the way.

Or students can write from the point of view that the character is away and coming home. Students need to determine where the character was when away and then what he or she will face on the way home. Students can create a similar plot structure that has a beginning, a middle, and an end with a problem to be solved by a character in the story. Students can be asked by others why their character went on the journey.

Students can use any of the following stories in which characters go on a journey, for ideas. For grades K–3:

Ada, Alma Flor. *The Gold Coin*.
Choi, Sook Nyul. *Yunmi and Halmoni's Trip*.
Goble, Paul. *The Girl Who Loved Wild Horses: A Native American Tale*.
Goble, Paul. *Star Boy*.
González-Jensen, Margarita. *The Butterfly Pyramid*.
Medearis, Angela Shelf. *The Singing Man: Adapted from a West African Folktale*.
Say, Allen. *Grandfather's Journey*.
Say, Allen. *The Lost Lake*.
Steptoe, John. *Mufaro's Beautiful Daughters: An African Tale*.
Steptoe, John. *The Story of Jumping Mouse: A Native American Legend*.

For grades 4 and up:

Curtis, Christopher Paul. *The Watsons Go to Birmingham—1963*.
McKay, Lawrence. *Journey Home* (To Vietnam).
Paterson, Katherine. *Jip: His Story*.
Sneve, Virginia Driving Hawk. *Jimmy Yellow Hawk*.
Soto, Gary. *Summer on Wheels*.
Taylor, Mildred D. *The Road to Memphis*.
Temple, Frances. *Grab Hands and Run*.
Uchida, Yoshiko. *Journey Home*.
Uchida, Yoshiko. *Sea of Gold and Other Tales from Japan*.

Story Quilt

After reading Deborah Hopkinson's *Sweet Clara and the Freedom Quilt*, have students create a paper story quilt of big squares to place in the room. By dividing the quilt among student groups, you can have students come up with scenes, pictures, symbols, or descriptive words that relate to the story's plot. The quilt can have the same title as the story. Colored paper, using colors from the story, can be used to fill in the rest of the quilt in an arranged pattern. Other titles for quilt stories can be found in chapter 2.

Brainstorming for Plot Elements and Cause and Effect

Below are various ideas for plot brainstorming to use with individual or groups of students.

- Broken-down car, broken-down school bus, broken swing, broken bicycle, broken scooter, broken skateboard
- Tired mom, tired dad, tired kid, tired brother, tired sister
- Fears of being alone, fears of being in the dark
- A big race, a lost animal, a lost important object

You could have available some books that deal with these topics. Ed Young's *Cat and Rat: The Legend of the Chinese Zodiac* is a good one to use about races and to answer the question of why cats and rats are enemies today.

Questions to ask students are who, what, where, when, how, and finally why for each idea that they discuss. After brainstorming ideas for plots, students write their own stories, focusing on cause and effect.

Writing Cause and Effect in Myths and Legends

Many myths try to explain natural phenomena or how things came to be a certain way. Something caused a change, resulting in a certain effect. Possible book titles to use include:

Goble, Paul. *The Great Race of the Birds and Animals* or *The Legend of the White Buffalo Woman.*

McGuire-Turcotte, Casey A. *How Honu the Turtle Got His Shell* (Hawaiian).

Flow Chart on Plot with Character

Ask students to create a flow chart for the stories that they read, for example with the following entries: Character I, Character II, Problem, Attempts to solve, and Solution.

Beginnings: The Hook

To assist students with getting a beginning of the story that can "hook" the reader, use newspaper headlines. Have students write the first paragraph after the headline. The title for their brief work may be taken from the headlines.

Students write their own "hooks" for their stories at the beginning. It could be a question, a piece of dialogue, or a description that sets a mood.

Beginnings, Middles, and Ends

Give students the beginning and middle, middle and end, or beginning and end of a folktale. Have them write the missing section. Students will need to understand character, setting, and plot (sequence of events with a problem, a climax or turning point, and a conclusion). Students may read their sections as you or other students read the sections that are unchanged. Post beginnings, middles, and ends on a wall with the rest of the folktale.

Rewriting the Ending of Stories: Modeling on the Experts

Using a book from one of the authors listed in this or earlier chapters that you have read aloud or that students have read, ask students to rewrite the ending. Students can share their endings in small groups or with a partner and then talk about how their ending is different from the one that is in the book. All endings can be posted in the classroom for students to read. The title above the postings can read: *Changing the Endings*.

Art and Writing: Cartoon Strip Creation

From a book that you have read as a class, or that students have read on their own, have students create a comic strip that shows an event in the story. Character, setting, and plot should be part of the strip. Characters can speak or think through balloons. Students can share their comic strips. They can be posted in sequence on a wall if they are from the same story, or if they are from different stories, they can be posted as individual creations with the title of the tale.

Using Visuals/Art to Show Characters in Scenes

Using a book that all students have read, have students draw a portrait of one character on one half of a piece of paper folded vertically and then write what the character does in a specific scene on the right side. Post the characters and scenes in the order in which they occur in the story.

CHAPTER 5

Through Whose Eyes
Is the Story Told? Point of View

POINT OF VIEW OF THE NARRATOR

In children's literature, the most common points of view in fictional stories are first-person and third-person limited. However, students may read stories written from an omniscient point of view, where stories give you an all-knowing point of view.

First-Person Narration

If all information from a story reaches readers from one point of view, where a main narrator tells us everything through a *persona*, labeled as "I" in the story, then that story is in first-person point of view. Readers are inside one "character's" head in the story—hearing, seeing, tasting, smelling, and feeling from that one character's point of view. Readers are as close to the main character as they can get in thoughts, speech, and action.

When young readers become writers, they need to be able to create this closeness to the reader. One way to do that is by creating characters from their own real worlds that they know very well. Walter Dean Myers draws from the real world for many of his books. Based on real people, the characters are shown through thoughts, speech, and actions in specific settings.

Question: "How did you decide on the point of view for *Me, Mop, and the Moondance Kid* and the sequel *Mop, Moondance, and the Nagasaki Knights*?"

Walter Dean Myers: "My son, the illustrator Christopher Myers (*Black Cat*, *Wings*, *Monster*), was not a very good Little League player although he considered himself to be a star in the making. He became the narrator of *Me, Mop, and the Moondance Kid*. My interest in foster children (Dean is the name of my foster parents) became the key to my interest in the story along with my son's baseball misadventures."[1]

For some authors, making the decision to tell a story from a particular point of view involves a weighing and balancing, trying to write it from one character's point of view, and then making a change to another character's point of view as the story takes shape. Mildred D. Taylor clarifies this struggle in her writing of *Song of the Trees*:

One story in particular kept nagging at me, a story my father had once told me about the cutting of some beloved trees on our family land. I attempted to write it from the grandmother's point of view without success. Gradually as I struggled, new twists to the story began to emerge. At last I decided to tell it through the eyes of Cassie Logan, a spirited eight year old.[2]

With Cassie telling this story, dramatic immediacy gathers readers in to share in the adventures that take place in *Song of the Trees*.

First-Person Narration with Two Characters

Some first-person narration stories may have two or more characters telling you the story, but each one is still told through the "I" point of view. One way to have two characters tell a story is to have the two characters "tell" their version of what is happening with alternating chapters. In children's literature, *two* first-person points of view in one story are uncommon. But there are some stories with two or more than two points of view using first-person narration. In *Dear Peter Rabbit* and *Yours Truly, Goldilocks*, Alma Flor Ada has many characters writing letters to each other. They all speak to readers, giving their first-person point of view on what is going on through their letters.

Third-Person Limited

This point of view gives us characters referred to by name or as "he," "she," or "they." This point of view is the most common one used in children's and young adult literature. Gary Soto writes his stories through third-person point of view.

Question: "How do you decide on who, inside your stories, will tell the story?"

Gary Soto: "I feel comfortable writing stories and novels for young people that are written in third person. For me, first person rings false; it's as if I'm the main character when I'm not. Now the issue of getting into the character's mind is impossible to answer since I don't know how the creative process works. How is it that musicians know where and when to fit their fingers on the keys to a saxophone? Or a piano? Magic happens when I write and the less I know about the process the better."[3]

In Virginia Driving Hawk Sneve's *The Chichi Hoohoo Bogeyman*, a third-person narration flows through the story, as readers "see" through the eyes of Mary Jo, a young girl who is of Sioux and Caucasian ancestry.

Question: "How did you decide what point of view you would use in *The Chichi Hoohoo Bogeyman*?"

Virginia Driving Hawk Sneve: "The book was inspired by my own family. My two Santee Dakota cousins—one married a Lakota woman (Chichi) and the other married a Hopi woman (Hoohoo), and me who married a Caucasian (Bogeyman). I told the story from the point of view of the latter, which is what my own children would have known."[4]

Likewise, Alma Flor Ada has written many of her stories, such as *My Name Is María Isabel*, in third-person point of view. In *My Name Is María Isabel*, the story is told by María. It is a third-person point of view, but readers might think that the title with the word "My" as the first word means that the story is being told with María telling the whole story (first-person narration). It's clear to readers, however, that what is going on in María's mind and what María is thinking and feeling in her world are communicated in a limited way. Readers know more because other characters tell us things as does the narrator's voice, the author operating behind the scenes. The title captures the irony—the expectations of María conflicting with those of the teacher, as she wishes to be called "María Isabel," rather than "Mary."

Alma Flor Ada poignantly conveys this confusion and loss of identity for María in one scene in particular. Readers find out that there are three Marías in the classroom. The teacher persists in calling María Isabel Lopez "Mary." María, confused and bewildered by an unknown name, daydreams about where she used to live in Puerto Rico and thinks about the family member for whom she was named in the first place. Because she is not included in the classroom with a name she recognizes, she does not hear the teacher call on her:

> "I'm talking to you, Mary." The teacher was now right by her desk, looking at María Isabel with a mix of surprise and impatience. María Isabel slumped down in her seat and looked at the dolphin that leaped across the cover of her book. She didn't know how to tell the teacher that she just didn't recognize herself in that strange name.[5]

The quest for recognition of cultural heritage through the acceptance of a name gives a unique multicultural, yet universal perspective to the story.

> Question: "How did you come up with the story idea for *My Name Is María Isabel*?"
>
> Alma Flor Ada: "*My Name Is María Isabel* comes in part from personal experience. My name was chosen by my grandmother. Her intent was that it would be only one word: *almaflor*. Unfortunately, the register officials enforced a two-word spelling. Nevertheless, I was told to write it as one word, and was always called by the whole name—until third grade. There, a well-intended teacher decided to inform me what my 'official name' was and proceeded to call me Alma. I felt alienated (Alma was my mother's name, not mine), but I was unable to say anything and just complied.
>
> "The passage in the book where the child feels the sadness of the way her mother used to write her name in her notebooks is very real. But probably I would never have written the book had I not realized that this was the story of many people. On beginning my work in bilingual education, I realized that many people had their names anglicized and did not feel the strength to claim their identity. And *María Isabel* came to be. Later, many people have approached me to tell me I had written their parents' story, their sister's story, or their own story, the story of someone they knew.
>
> "The story is thus very personal, and yet universal. Names are important throughout the world, but whenever there has been colonialism of

any sort, people have had their names changed, and they have internal-
ized that the names of the colonizer have more strength, more power."[6]

Readers understand María's dilemma—that she has to figure out what
to say or do to let the teacher know how she thinks and feels about being called "Mary." Readers see her becoming stronger and more confi-
dent and clearer in what she wants, solving her problem in her quest for
a clear, defined identity that she wants for her own.

Two Third-Person Limited Points of View in One Story

Young writers could also use two different characters to tell a story.
Joseph Bruchac creates two third-person points of view that alternate in
the story to reinforce the theme in the work, which is respect and tolerance:

> Respect also involves tolerance and seeing the world through the eyes of
> others. My novel *Arrow over the Door* is written from two points of
> view, that of a Quaker boy in a Meeting House and that of an Abenaki
> boy who is part of a scouting party working for the British just before the
> Battle of Saratoga. When these two sides finally meet there is a moment
> of great tension, when the wrong move might result in bloodshed. But,
> instead the two sides realize that they have much in common and they
> end up relating to each other in peace. [7]

Three Points of View

The Iktomi "trickster" stories from Native American lore by Paul
Goble have three points of view: Iktomi (in his thoughts), Iktomi (as a
character, third-person limited), and then an unusual point of view (ad-
dressing the reader throughout the story to ask the reader to take part in
the story).

> Question: "Would you talk about the three points of view in the Iktomi
> 'trickster' stories?"
> Paul Goble: "Iktomi stories are familiar to everyone. In telling, every-
> one knew what was coming next. The joy was in good storytelling and
> laughing at the joker. In the oral tradition, listeners could interject their

thoughts and ideas about Iktomi. This is not easy in books, but I included asides and questions for the reader to engage the listeners. Iktomi's thoughts in the small type are what I think he might be thinking. Listeners and readers can add their own ideas."[8]

HOW DO YOUNG WRITERS DECIDE WHAT POINT OF VIEW TO USE?

Questions about characters and events can help young writers decide which point of view to use.

- Are there one or more characters that are essential to the story plot line and need to have their thoughts, dialogues, and action as part of the story? If so, then third-person limited POV, using character names and "he/she" and "they" is the choice for point of view.
- Should a main character know and relate everything that happens? If that kind of narration fits the story, then first-person POV is the only way that you can convey through the "eyes" of one person all of what takes place in a story.

SETTING, CHARACTER, AND PLOT IN RELATION TO POINT OF VIEW

The point of view chosen by the writer communicates elements of setting, character, and plot to the reader. One story for you to use to show the connection of setting, character, and plot to point of view is Alma Flor Ada's *The Rooster Who Went to His Uncle's Wedding*.

Here, in the third-person limited point of view, is the first paragraph from *The Rooster Who Went to His Uncle's Wedding*:

> Early one morning, when the sun had not yet appeared, the rooster of this story was busy shining his beak and combing his feathers. It was the day of his uncle's wedding, and the rooster wanted to be on time.[9]

Point of View and Character

This story is told in third person with the rooster established as the main character. His "wants" are clear and he values two things: being on time and looking great for the wedding celebration. Readers align with the character, his values, his concern for looking good for the uncle's wedding—problems and events that shape his life or that he shapes.

Point of View and Setting

The time is clearly established as before sunrise. We also know it is a special day for the rooster. Because the story is a folktale, the setting for it is a backdrop and explained briefly, without much description. Again, the colorful Aztec illustrations portray much more of the setting than the written tale.

Point of View and Plot

While readers don't know from the first paragraph what will happen yet, they do know that the rooster wants to be on time. The beginning of a problem or conflict is tentative. What if something happens to him so that he can't be on time? It does. Because he has not eaten, he succumbs to eating a kernel of corn covered in mud, and his beak becomes dirty. The tale flows on with the rooster going through a cumulative series of events to become clean again and presentable for the wedding.

BACKGROUND CONNECTIONS AND FOLKTALES

Some books that Alma Flor Ada writes, such as *The Rooster Who Went to His Uncle's Wedding*, reflect the Cuban surroundings of her Latin American childhood. Alma Flor's grandmother told this story, and Alma Flor has retold it in the printed form of a picture storybook in both English and Spanish. Her childhood in Cuba, rich in the opportunity to hear stories, enriched her own storytelling ability. Others that she writes reflect Northern European folktales that she became acquainted with in her childhood, such as those tales that are woven through *Dear Peter Rabbit* and *Yours Truly, Goldilocks*.[10]

Just as I used a first paragraph from a story above as an example, you could read or have students read first paragraphs from many different books to help them understand how the literary element of point of view, like others, is introduced so early in the story. Those first paragraphs could also be used as models for young writers as they learn how to write from different points of view.

WHAT IF A WRITER WANTS TO CHANGE POINT OF VIEW?

Even though a writer may choose to write from one point of view when starting a story, he or she may decide while writing that the character chosen to tell the story is not the one through whose "eyes" the story should be told. That means, then, that young writers need to know that they may have to switch from first- to third- or third- to first-person point of view if one type of narration isn't working to tell a particular story. The writer changes point of view to meet character needs or story events.

Activities that follow connect the writer to point of view in a variety of ways, from identification of point of view to practice in writing from various points of view.

Journal Activity: Character Sketch

Have students write their own character sketch of a favorite character from a first-person point of view. "I" written with a capital letter is an important English convention. You could review that convention with very young writers.

Identification and Assessment

Choose a variety of multicultural children's literature that you have read aloud or that students have read on their own to identify points of view. Ask students to list titles, point of view, and the characters through whose point of view the stories are told. The following is an example:

Author: Ada
Title: *The Rooster Who Went to His Uncle's Wedding*
Point of view: Third person
Through character/narrator: Author through narrator and rooster

The following list includes possible book choices. For first-person point of view for grades K–3:

Ada, Alma Flor. *Dear Peter Rabbit.*
Ada, Alma Flor. *Yours Truly, Goldilocks.*
Medearis, Angela Shelf. *Dancing with the Indians.*
Say, Allen. *Grandfather's Journey.*

For grades 4 and up:

Curtis, Christopher Paul. *Bud, Not Buddy.*
Myers, Walter Dean. *Won't Know Until I Get There.*
Orlev, Uri. *Lydia, Queen of Palestine.*
Salisbury, Graham. *The Blue Skin of the Sea.*
Taylor, Mildred D. *The Friendship.*
Temple, Frances. *Grab Hands and Run.*

For third-person point of view for grades K–3:

Begay, Shonto. *Ma'ii and Cousin Horned Toad.*
De San Souci, Robert. *The Talking Eggs: A Folktale from the American South.*
Kimmel, Eric. *Anansi and the Magic Stick.*
Say, Allen. *Allison.*
Soto, Gary. *Chato's Kitchen.*
Soto, Gary. *Off and Running.*

For third-person point of view for grades 4 and up:

Bruchac, Joseph. *The Arrow over the Door.*
Paterson, Katherine. *Jip: His Story.*
Soto, Gary. *Summer on Wheels.*
Taylor, Mildred D. *Roll of Thunder, Hear My Cry.*
Yep, Laurence. *Child of the Owl.*
Yep, Laurence. *The Amah.*

Multicultural Connections to Expand Understanding of Stories

Read aloud one of the chapters from Alma Flor Ada's *Where the Flame Trees Bloom* or *Under the Royal Palms*. For example, read the chapter "The Rag Dolls" aloud. Have on the board or computer the following questions ahead of time. They may be answered individually, in a small group, or in a large group.

- Who is the main person in this story from Alma Flor Ada's childhood?
- Where does the story take place?
- What does Alma Flor Ada tell you about her great grandmother?
- Why is the grandmother making the dolls?
- What point of view is used in the story?
- How do you know that this story takes place in a tropical setting?

Ask students to write a short sketch from their own point of view, using "I" to tell about someone they know from their family, a friend, or someone in their community who makes objects that he or she gives to others. Have students share what they write with members of a group or the class.

Identifying Characters and Writing about Them through the First-Person Point of View

Ask students to choose one character from a favorite story and write a letter to another character in the same story or another story. As they pretend to be the character, they use "I" to show point of view. Questions to ask may be placed on the board/overhead/computer. Following are some sample questions. For you, as a character in the story:

- What do you do in the story?
- How do you do it?
- Why do you do it?
- Where do you go or stay in the story?
- Why are you in the story?

For you, as the student writer: How do you feel about the character to whom you are writing? Students should answer: "I feel. . . . Why?"

A Visual Understanding of Point of View Using Cartoons

Use cartoons to illustrate point of view. You will need cartoon characters from newspapers, which students can provide.

Identifying Thoughts and Dialogue. Have students look at cartoon balloons for thoughts and balloons for speech and dialogue to identify whether a cartoon character is thinking or speaking in a frame. Use overhead projectors or computer scanners for discussion.

Reviewing the Same Cartoon Character for Thoughts and Dialogue. Use cartoons in which the same character is shown in two pictures: one in which he or she is thinking and one in which he or she is talking. Ask students the following question: How do balloons work to show a character's point of view—in his or her thoughts or speech?

Creating a Visual Example of Point of View. Have students draw two cartoon characters, each with a balloon. One balloon will be for the thoughts of one character and the other will be a balloon for speech. Have students create the words for both speech and thought and place them in the balloons. In small groups, ask students to review their cartoons, answering the following questions: Who is speaking and why? Who is listening or thinking and why?

Thoughts and Dialogue in Point of View

Choose multicultural stories with differing points of view. After reading one from first-person and one from third-person points of view, ask students to respond to these questions in small groups:

- Who is telling the story?
- Whose feelings, thoughts, speech, or actions do you see?
- What examples can you give for those feelings, thoughts, speech, or actions?
- Do you think anyone else in the story could tell the story just as well? Who? Why? What would they have to do to be able to tell it as well?

Modeling after the Experts

Writing First-Person Point of View. Have students work in pairs to rewrite a paragraph or page from a multicultural children's literature book that is in third-person and change it to first-person point of view.

Writing Third-Person Point of View. Have students work in pairs to rewrite a paragraph or page from a multicultural book that is in first-person and change it to third-person point of view. Students will need to identify the point of view of stories first. A sample visual can be filled in by the class or individual students and can be posted while students work. Ask the following discussion questions after students have completed their paragraphs:

- What did you have to do to change the point of view of the paragraph or page you were working on?
- Why do you think that the author wrote the story in the original point of view?

Staying in a First-Person Point of View

Have older students examine a page that is first-person point of view and then write the story from another first-person point of view, using another character of their choice.

Setting and Third-Person Point of View

Ask students to write a brief description of a setting with a character in it, using third person, a name or names, or "he/she/him/her" for that character and others in the story in description or narration.

Using the Position in Setting to Show Point of View

Focus on Position of Place of Character to Enrich Point of View. Using various scenes from multicultural stories and the characters within the story, change the point of view and perspective in the story to another character's point of view by actually changing the position from where the story is viewed. An example follows from Eric Kimmel's *Anansi Goes Fishing*:

Title: *Anansi Goes Fishing*
Character: Turtle; Location: By the river

Character: Bird; Flying over, looking down
Character: Alligator; Location: In river looking at turtle

Have students draw, draw/write, or write the scene below. Here is an example to use to show changes to think about in perspective/position in telling a story.

A breakfast table from the point of view of a dog below a table
or a child sitting at a table
or a mouse on top of a cupboard

Comparisons of Point of View

Using a version of *The Three Little Pigs* and Jon Scieszka's *The True Story of the 3 Little Pigs!*, ask students to tell you whose story is being told and how. This activity becomes a way to see the difference between two extremely different points of view—that of the pigs and that of the wolf.

Have students write a story from the point of view of a character who does not get to tell the story, but could, such as the baby bear in any version of *Goldilocks and the Three Bears*, one of the two dolls in "Barbie" from Gary Soto's *Baseball in April and Other Stories*, or the bus driver from Mildred D. Taylor's *Roll of Thunder, Hear My Cry*.

Character Sketch

Ask students to write their own character sketches of their favorite characters as if they were the characters. They will need to use "I"—first-person narration—for their chosen characters.

Setting and Third-Person Narration

Ask students to write a brief setting description with a character in it, using third-person narration.

CHAPTER 6

How Writers Express Feelings: Tone

Tone is the attitude of a writer toward the subject that he or she is writing about. Readers "hear" the tone of the overall story, presented by the writer of that story. The writer shows what he or she believes and feels about the whole story within the story, which gives readers a chance to have a particular response to the story. If the writer is successful with tone, readers see the story in the tone that the author intended, such as humorous, serious, sentimental, ironic, straightforward, optimistic, or pessimistic.

Overall tone may be expressed through thoughts, speech, action, or description by the author's words in the story or any narrator who may be a main character or minor character.

Readers are aware of the way the author thinks and feels—positive or negative—about the subject or the whole story. And readers are also aware of the actual characters themselves and what they think or feel, whether they are positive or negative about someone or something happening in the story.

In an interview, Allen Say reveals the way an author thinks about his subject and the overall tone of his books.

Martha Davis Beck: "In your books, there is a tension between stillness and restlessness, satisfaction and longing."

Allen Say: "There's a concept I discovered through painting and fly fishing: that things happen on the edges. When you're fishing for trout, the fish holds between the fast current and the slow current. I view life that way. Tension is form."[1]

TONE WITHIN A STORY

Within a story, particular tones or tensions reflect individual characters. For example, the voice of each character can tell us more about how readers are supposed to think and feel about a character. In that voice, tone makes aspects of character more "believable" to us. Characters see in others or feel in themselves such emotions as love, hatred, sadness, anger, fear, envy, jealousy, happiness, loneliness, embarrassment, or even exuberance. Readers "hear" these emotions and tone through characters' voices in the story.

When young writers move from the role of readers to writers, they need to consider how they are going to convey any of these tones to the reader. Because they can't hear the "voices" actually spoken, young writers need to use words to show the manner of speech of different characters. Those words convey attitudes or emotions (feelings) of what is positive or negative to a character or characters. Learning to create these emotional connections is important for young writers because they will want the readers of their stories to align with characters and their adventures, and "buy into" going along with the characters in the story.

In *The First Strawberries: A Cherokee Story*, Joseph Bruchac, through the narrator, shows a description of tone in action:

> Now the Sun tried a third time. Where its beams touched the Earth, blackberries grew up. They were dark and plump, but the woman's anger was too great and she did not see them.[2]

In that excerpt, readers see the anger and feel the tension in the story through the narration and description of action.

TOO MUCH OF A GOOD THING

As mentioned in chapter 2, the word that is used most often to show a character speaking is the word *said*. If writers wanted to use words to show humor, sarcasm, happiness, or anger, they could add any of those words to "said" so that the dialogue would read, "said sarcastically," "said happily," or "said angrily." But those tacked-on adverbs don't show anger. Rather, young writers should show how people act to show that they are sarcastic, happy, or angry. Young writers need to be aware of how to create "tone" in a story because descriptions of actions show feelings more dramatically. By showing tone through narration and action as Bruchac does in *The First Strawberries*, rather than describing it by using an adverb attached in the tag line, writers will create a better sense of tone in the story.

WHAT'S SO FUNNY?

Making a story funny requires young writers to be able to "see" humorous characters or situations that make readers smile or laugh. Laurence Yep comments on why a sense of humor is important in his writing of children's books, especially in *The Imp That Ate My Homework*: "Because life without humor isn't worth living. Our sense of humor gives us perspective on our world and most importantly on our place in it."[3]

Young writers need to understand the power of different tones in multicultural literature so that they will have models for figuring out tone in their own stories.

They also need to understand that their characters must show feelings. What readers know about those feelings is determined by whom the writer chooses to tell the story. Then tone and point of view, expressed through thoughts, speech, action, and description, come together to illuminate the story.

> Question: "How did you decide on point of view for the *Magic Paintbrush*?"
> Laurence Yep: "The emotional center was the boy."[4]

The narrator in this story is "the boy." In any story, "the emotional center" is the tone expressed by the writer that is most important to convince readers to go along with the characters in the story.

STRATEGIES FOR UNDERSTANDING TONE

Following are strategies to assist students with understanding tone in multicultural children's literature. The various activities with tone can help you pick the most appropriate for the students with whom you are working.

Journal Activity

Ask students to make a two-column page in their journals for "Tone." In one column, they can place the heading *Title* and in the other column the question: "How Does the Title Show the Tone of the Story?" Students write the responses to different story titles. They may share these written responses in pairs or in small groups.

Assessment: Identifying Tone

Using a variety of multicultural books, students will identify different emotional tones as expressed by individual characters in the books. The books under each "tone" are suggested to go with the activities.

Anger/Resentment, or Meanness as Feelings of Characters. This activity illustrates how anger is shown in a story and how angry feelings are calmed. Following are questions to ask students:

- Why is the main character angry?
- How did the anger disappear? Or what made the anger disappear?
- Was there a time when you were angry or afraid?
- What happened?
- How did you solve the problem, or was it solved by someone else or something else that happened?

Included in the following list are books appropriate for grades K–3:

Bruchac, Joseph. *The First Strawberries: A Cherokee Story.*
Hol, Colby. *The Birth of the Moon.*
Paterson, Katherine. *The Smallest Cow in the World.*
Paterson, Katherine. *The Tale of the Mandarin Ducks.*
Say, Allen. *Emma's Rug.*
Steptoe, John. *Stevie.*

For grades 4 and up:

Paterson, Katherine. *Flip-Flop Girl*.
Soto, Gary. "Barbie" in *Baseball in April and Other Stories*.
Yep, Laurence. *Ribbons*.
Yep, Laurence. *The Amah*.

Humor in a Story. After reading aloud or having students read the letters from Alma Flor Ada's *Dear Peter Rabbit*, ask students what the tone of the story is. Extend discussions as you work with students. Ask the following questions: What makes this book funny? Why do you laugh? Following are several books to use with this activity. For grades K–3:

Ada, Alma Flor. *Dear Peter Rabbit*.
Ada, Alma Flor. *Yours Truly Goldilocks*.
Kimmel, Eric. *Anansi Goes Fishing*.
Kimmel, Eric. *The Chanukkah Guest*.
Lester, Julius. *Sam and the Tigers: A New Telling of* Little Black Sambo.
Soto, Gary. *Chato's Kitchen*.
Young, Ed. *Donkey Trouble*.

For grades 4 and up:

Curtis, Christopher Paul. *The Watsons Go to Birmingham—1963*.
Curtis, Christopher Paul. *Bud, Not Buddy*.
Kimmel, Eric. *Website of the Warped Wizard*.
Myers, Walter Dean. *Me, Mop, and the Moondance Kid*.
Myers, Walter Dean. *Mop, Moondance, and the Nagasaki Knights*.
Orlev, Uri. *Lydia, Queen of Palestine*.
Yep, Laurence. *The Case of the Goblin Pearls*.
Yep, Laurence. *The Case of the Missing Ruby and Other Stories*.
Yep, Laurence. *Cockroach Cooties*.
Yep, Laurence. *The Imp That Ate My Homework*.

Fear in a Story. Ask students to make lists of the scenes that are "scary" or that make them feel "uneasy" in the story. Discuss with students how the author resolves these scary incidents. Ask students the following question: What happens in the story to get rid of the tension or "scary feelings" that you have as a reader? Following are some appropriate books for grades K–3:

Aardema, Verna. *Jackal's Flying Lesson: A Khoikhoi Tale*.
Kimmel, Eric. *Sirko and the Wolf: A Ukranian Tale*.
Young, Ed. *Lon Po Po: A Red-Riding Hood Story from China*.

For grades 4 and up:

McKissack, Patricia C. *The Dark Thirty: Southern Tales of the Supernatural*.
Medearis, Angela Shelf. *Haunts: Five Hair-Raising Tales*.
Medearis, Angela Shelf. *The Ghost of Sifty-Sifty Sam*.
Orlev, Uri. *The Island on Bird Street*.
Paterson, Katherine. *Jip: His Story*.
Paterson, Katherine. *The Great Gilly Hopkins*.
Polacco, Patricia. *Picnic at Mudsock Meadow*.

Happiness/Joy or Overcoming Sadness in a Story. With any of the books listed below that you have read with students or they have read on their own, ask students to discuss the following questions:

- If the story has a satisfied or happy tone at the end, why is that so?
- If the story has a sad tone at the end, why is that so?
- Is there sadness in the story and still a resolved/comfortable tone at the end? Why?

For grades K–3:

González-Jensen, Margarita. *The Butterfly Pyramid*.
Myers, Walter Dean. *The Blues of Flats Brown*.
Young, Ed. *The Lost Horse*.

For grades 4 and up:

Goble, Paul. *Love Flute*.
Taylor, Mildred D. *Mississippi Bridge*.
Yep, Laurence. *Ribbons*.

Assessment: Selecting the Tone of a Story

Read a humorous book aloud. Have students make a class list of why they think a book you have read aloud is funny. Ask students to determine what kind of tone is in the story. Use the chart below to mark "X" for tone, and ask the students to give reasons for their answers.

Give students in grades K–6 picture storybooks with different tones (all grades) and ask them to review the books for tone. Students add their titles and place an "X" for the tone that is most appropriate for the story. They then explain to the class why they chose that tone, using an example to back up their choice of tone.

Title
Scary tone
Funny tone
Happy tone
Sad tone
Other tone

Use the following summary statement with any of the above tones: The funny, sad, sarcastic, or embarrassing tone (the one that is your focus) can be shown through pictures or written in the storyline and seen in description, thoughts, speech, or action.

Understanding Character Feelings from the Story

After reading aloud any story, or having students read their own stories that they have written, place the following questions on the board, overhead, or computer:

- Who is the main character?
- What feelings does this character show in the story? How?
- Who is a minor character?
- What feelings does this character show in the story? How?

Give one example for each character.

Identifying Tone in Greeting Cards

Bring in an assortment of greeting cards that have different tones in them. Simple ones can work for younger students. Have students identify the tone in each one: sad, happy, funny, serious. Then have students create their own greeting card by hand, on the computer, or from a computer greeting card Web site, choosing one to fit the tone they wish. Have members of the class identify the tone of the other students' cards.

Creating Tone and Story from Objective Information

Give students a scenario such as the one below that supplies them with basic information. Have the students rewrite the paragraph to have a character in a story with a certain tone throughout the paragraph. Students may choose from funny, sad, serious, happy, or joyful.

For grades K–3, use the following scenario: Your main character is named Sophie Wilson or Sam Wilson. Sam or Sophie wants a new toy. You decide what toy that is. But Sam or Sophie can't have it because he or she doesn't have any money. He or she won't steal it. Someone else wants the toy and tries to keep Sophie or Sam from getting it. What is one funny, scary, sad, or happy thing that could happen to him or her next? Write the next scene with Sophie or Sam in it.

For grades 4 and up, use the following scenario: Your main character is named Harley Donovan or Hanna Donovan. He or she is a private eye but not very good. He or she likes to eat pizza in his or her car. Harley or Hanna is going to the scene of the crime—a place that serves only ice cream. The electrical power has gone out, and the ice cream is starting to melt. What is one funny, scary, sad, or happy thing that could happen to him or her next? Write the next scene with Harley or Hanna in it.

Buddy/Grouping Activity on Tone

Have students partner and read the same picture book. Ask them to find one passage or section that shows the tone of the book. The partners will read their passage aloud to a larger group and other students will identify the tone of their passages.

Assessment: Dialogue

Ask students to write at least five sentences of dialogue with two characters talking, one of which shows a particular tone. Students can use jokes that they know, or make up the characters and the dialogue scene. They then can identify the tone that they created by writing the dialogue and tone on a poster board for the classroom.

Tone throughout the Book

To show authorial tone throughout a whole book, compare two different books with the same themes but with different tones. See chapter 7, "What the Story Is Really About: Theme," for books with similar themes.

Film Watch

Have students watch sections of a multicultural film that shows a certain mood with picture and sound. Then have them watch just the picture and no sound. Ask them the following question: How does the music set the tone for different scenes?

Then have students listen to the sound and voices of the film without the picture. Ask them the following: How does the picture make the meaning clearer with the tone of the voices and/or music?

Creating Tone through Sound

Using musical instruments or recordings, have students design background music for a scene from a book that they have read. Have students write on 3×5 cards why the music works for the scene that they chose to match to the tone of the scene in the story. Students should be able to describe the tone as mysterious, happy, sad, eerie, humorous, funny, or other descriptive words of their choice.

Colors and Feelings in a Story

Ask students to think of colors that could represent tones of a story that you have read aloud or they have read on their own. Have them figure out when the tone changes—such as from sad to happy or serious to funny. You can use water and mix primary food colors to show feelings. For instance, if a character is blue and unhappy, students might use the blue to show that feeling. If a character's feelings change, then the colors should change too. Ask students to back up the colors they chose by being able to explain how the color shows feelings or changes in feelings.

On the Way through a Story

When reading a serious or sad part of a story, discuss with students what the author did with the characters, setting, or plot to make them, as readers, feel that way. Ask students what they think will happen next with the tone of the story.

Setting Can Show Tone

When reading a story that has a setting that shows a mood, ask students in small groups to discuss how the mood from a setting reflects what happens to the characters. How does it affect the plot?

Have students write a brief setting that shows mood or tone with character and beginning plot.

Assessment: Tone in Pictures

Collect as many pictures of people, animals, and places as possible that show different tones. Give students in groups a variety of pictures with different tones, such as happy, sad, serious, funny, angry, afraid. Have students work in small groups to identify the tone of each picture. Check students' knowledge by asking group leaders to hold up the pictures and present the choice for the tone of the picture decided on by the group.

Illustrations Can Show Tone

Using picture books of your choice, have student pairs look at the illustrations to determine how they show the tone of the story. Have students share their findings in groups of four.

CHAPTER 7

What the Story Is Really About: Theme

Theme is the overall message in a story. Readers walk away from a story with a theme or meaning that goes beyond the storyline and reflects what it means to be human. *Love*, *coping with a loss*, *self-identity*, *growing up*, *overcoming fears*, or *courage* are themes that briefly convey the overall meaning of stories.

A theme reflects what it means to be human, what it means to be alive and capable of reason and emotion. A theme is the central idea— a message that defines us as human beings.

Some authors decide on a theme before writing. Others write and a theme emerges from the writing. Still others write and really don't seem to be concerned with theme; they just write the stories. In the end, though, the readers are the ones to whom the theme is important. They take the theme and make meaning from the story for themselves, and, in doing so, gain some understanding about the universal connections that show our humanity.

AUTHORS SPEAK ABOUT THEMES

Overall themes, for some writers, are messages that flow through a story. Readers of that story won't necessarily see the words that are used to describe theme in the stories. Yet the meaning of those words takes shape through all of the literary elements of a story. For example, readers may not see words such as *respect* or *tolerance* written in a story, but they would see characters, plot, setting, point of view, and tone that all work together to show tolerance or respect. That a story has something important to say that goes beyond the story itself is an important fact to share with young readers.

Authors such as Joseph Bruchac, Virginia Driving Hawk Sneve, and Shonto Begay are aware of the themes that their books contain and they are adept at explaining them to us.

Question: "What do you consider to be a main theme in your books?"

Joseph Bruchac: "One of my major themes is respect—for yourself, for others, for all living things. Respect also involves tolerance and seeing the world through the eyes of others. My novel *Arrow over the Door* is written from two points of view, that of a Quaker boy in a Meeting House and that of an Abenaki boy who is part of a scouting party working for the British just before the Battle of Saratoga. When these two sides finally meet, there is a moment of great tension, when the wrong move might result in bloodshed. But, instead the two sides realize that they have much in common and they end up relating to each other in peace. Those linked themes of respect, tolerance, empathy, and peace turn up again and again in my writing—in *The Heart of a Chief*, in *Eagle Song*, and in *Sacajawea*."[1]

When Virginia Driving Hawk Sneve talks about theme, she makes the point that a theme develops over time out of writing. For her, themes are not conscious products of her mind when she's writing. Young writers need to be aware that theme develops as a story moves along, and that writers generally have similar themes in the books they write. Working with the same themes over time may give writers the impetus to keep writing, so that in their own work students can see what themes emerge from their stories over time.

Question: "Writers seem to have themes that cut across their works and appear again and again. If you had to express what your books were about, what would you say?"

Virginia Driving Hawk Sneve: "There was no conscious effort to have a similar theme in my fiction; but, on reflection, it is probably that the values and traditions of our historic past are still alive in contemporary life."[2]

Finally, Shonto Begay, Navaho writer and illustrator, talks about how the text and illustrations are important to show a theme of people being more alike than different.

Question: "What do you consider the main theme in your books?"

Shonto Begay: "As a Navaho, it is to share my world, visually and literally in words and pictures. Things get glossed over in other stories about Native Americans. Some people think of us in a highly romanticized way. But we live in the real world, with joys, hopes, and despairs. We are more alike than different."[3]

The underlying "theme" of the story is a result of interaction of character, setting, and plot, told through a particular point of view with a particular tone. What this all means is that young writers do not have to know the theme of a story before they write. What they have to know is what the story will be about. That is plot, not theme. Theme, the underlying meaning that makes the story have universal significance or appeal to many readers, becomes an act of understanding and perception for the readers, who read for story. Theme is a gift—a universal message through story.

Students can express themes in stories read by talking about them, using very specific words or phases. A story could be one about "fear" or "being afraid." More specifically, the story could be about coping with a kind of fear—fear of the dark, fear of failure, fear of being abandoned. A theme about the fear of abandonment, which appears in stories like *Hansel and Gretel*, might be the fear of the loss of parents and/or the fear of being left alone.

Themes of love and loss might take shape in coping with the loss of a relative or surviving a social conflict or war. How that survival takes place and is then written about becomes the action of memory, the power of imagination, and the narrative of story on the part of the author.

Writing about the Holocaust, Uri Orlev creates a worldview that readers may not know, but they know as soon as he tells them about it, and they are willing to go there with him. In going with him, they come away connected to a human experience with which they can identify. In that identification, insight and empathy allow readers to see from the other side, to empathize with and understand more deeply what went on in the Holocaust.

I remember many adventures that came our way because of the strange places we played in and the strange objects we found there—all sorts of things that one finds in the street only in wartime, like the barrel of a cannon which we exploded by mistake. Or a dead horse that opened its mouth. Or crazy Rubinstein who ran through the ghetto shouting in Yiddish, "Everyone's equal," as we ran around after him. I asked my mother what he meant and she answered that perhaps he was saying that all are equal in the face of death. That was when I wrote my first poem.[4]

The above statement from Uri Orlev contains the themes found in his books—courage and rites of passage. His stories are about growing up in a world tainted by war.

STRATEGIES FOR IDENTIFYING THEME

The following activities with theme give many choices of books to use. This list, like others in this book for your use, is not inclusive but suggestive, so that you may choose what is here, or use similar multicultural books with which you are familiar. You may find some short story collections with the short stories grouped by theme, such as Laurence Yep's *American Dragons: Twenty-five Asian American Voices*, in which identity or relationships with parents as themes are listed among others. While this particular book is more appropriate for young adults, it does show how one author groups stories by theme for readers.

Journal Activities

Themes in Stories. Have students divide a page into two columns with a vertical line. They label one column *Books Heard* and the other *Books Read on My Own*. Students list book title and theme, and write one or more sentences to explain why they think the theme fits that book.

Using One Theme to Focus on One Character. Using books with a particular theme, such as friendship, students can discuss or write about how theme is revealed through a character's thoughts, words, actions, or descriptions.

Theme Comparison/Discussion

Allen Say's books offer a way to look at themes connected with "journeys."

As a writer who grew up in Japan and moved to the United States when he was sixteen, Say speaks of his writing, dreams, and life journey: "I am trying to give shape to my dreams—the old business of making myths—the fundamental force of art. And so, *Grandfather's Journey* is essentially a dream book, for the life's journey is an endless dreaming of the places you've left behind and the places yet to be reached."[5]

One of the ways to become familiar with how themes work is to have students discuss and compare two books with a similar theme, such as *Grandfather's Journey* and another listed under journeys in the section below, to see how similar themes are treated differently. The following books, classified by theme, are from multicultural perspectives. The study of themes will give young writers a way of looking at their own writings. As they write more and more stories, they can review their own stories to see if they can identify themes there.

Journeys of Self-Discovery: Ada, Alma Flor. *The Gold Coin* (Hispanic); Curtis, Christopher Paul. *Bud, Not Buddy* (African American); Curtis, Christopher Paul. *The Watsons Go to Birmingham—1963* (African American); Goble, Paul. *The Girl Who Loved Wild Horses* (Native American); Myers, Walter Dean. *The Blues of Flats Brown* (African American); Say, Allen. *Grandfather's Journey* (Japanese); Soto, Gary. *Summer on Wheels* (Hispanic); Soto, Gary. *Pacific Crossing* (Hispanic); Steptoe, John. *The Story of Jumping Mouse: A Native American Legend*

Survival: Ada, Alma Flor. *My Name Is María Isabel* (Hispanic); Bruchac, Joseph. *Iroquois Stories: Heroes and Heroines, Monsters and Magic*; Cohen, Carol Lee, reteller. *The Mud Pony: A Traditional Skidi Pawnee Tale*. Illustrated by Shonto Begay; Demi. *One Grain of Rice: A Mathematical Folktale* (Indian); Lester, Julius. *Sam and the Tigers: A New Telling of* Little Black Sambo (African American); Lord, Betty Bao. *In the Year of the Boar and Jackie Robinson* (Chinese); Orlev, Uri. *The Island on Bird Street* (Jewish); Soto, Gary. *Chato's Kitchen* (Hispanic); Temple, Frances. *Grab Hands and Run* (Hispanic)

Fantasies, Dreams, and Changes: Casler, Leigh. *The Boy Who Dreamed of an Acorn*. Illustrated by Shonto Begay; Goble, Paul. *Love*

Flute (Native American); Hoffman, Mary. *Amazing Grace* (African American); Hoffman, Mary. *Boundless Grace* (daughter, father, stepmother); Lester, Julius. *Albidaro and the Mischievous Dream*; Polacco, Patricia. *Appelemando's Dream*; Say, Allen. *River Dream* (Japanese); Uchida, Yoshiko. *Jar of Dreams* (Japanese); Yep, Laurence. *The Butterfly Boy*; Yep, Laurence. *Tree of Dreams: Ten Tales from the Garden of Night* (Chinese); Young, Ed. *Night Visitors*

Family Relationships: Ada, Alma Flor. *My Name Is María Isabel* (daughter and parents); Castañeda, Omar. *Abuela's Weave* (grandmother and daughter); Choi, Sook Nyul. *Yunmi and Halmoni's Trip* (grandmother and granddaughter); Choi, Sook Nyul. *The Best Older Sister* (siblings); Curtis, Christopher Paul. *Bud, Not Buddy* (grandson and grandfather); González-Jensen, Margarita. *The Butterfly Pyramid* (son and mother); Guback, Georgia. *Luka's Quilt* (Hawaiian) (granddaughter and grandmother); Myers, Walter Dean. *Won't Know Until I Get There* (son and parents, foster brother); Orlev, Uri. *Lydia, Queen of Palestine*; Salisbury, Graham. *Jungle Dogs* (father and son); Say, Allen. *Allison* (daughter and parents); Say, Allen. *The Lost Lake* (father and son); Soto, Gary. *The Skirt* (mother and daughter); Steptoe, John. *My Daddy Is a Monster . . . Sometimes* (father, son, and daughter); Yep, Laurence. *Child of the Owl* (granddaughter and grandmother); Yep, Laurence. *Ribbons* (granddaughter and grandmother); Yep, Laurence. *The Amah* (mother and daughter)

Friendship or Coping with Losses: Ada, Alma Flor. *Friend Frog*; Bruchac, Joseph. *The First Strawberries: A Cherokee Story*; Carmi, Daniella. *Samir and Yonatan*; Goble, Paul. *Adopted by the Eagles*; Medearis, Angela Shelf. *The Adventures of Sugar and Junior*; Paterson, Katherine. *Bridge to Terabithia*; Say, Allen. *Stranger in the Mirror*; Soto, Gary. *Big Bushy Mustache*; Soto, Gary. *Off and Running*; Woodson, Jacqueline. *The Other Side*

Coping with Fears and Courage: Goble, Paul. *The Gift of the Sacred Dog*; Orlev, Uri. *The Island on Bird Street*; Uchida, Yoshiko. *The Bracelet*; Uchida, Yoshiko. *Journey to Topaz*

Art (Mobiles) and Theme

After reading a book aloud, have students construct a mobile in which the title is in the center, the theme below it, and characters dangling from the theme chosen. Or construct a mobile in which the author's name is in the center, with titles and themes from the author's books hanging below. The shapes for the mobile may be visuals that represent images from the story, such as clouds, trees, lightning, and so on.

Art (Posters) and Theme

Place five themes (some choices might be fear, friendship, family, peer groups, survival, acceptance, sense of self, or growing up) on large posters around the room. As you or students read multicultural books, write or have students write the title under the theme of the book. Since some books may have more than one theme, some book titles would be placed under more than one theme. Ask students to find sentences from the book to support their choices and write those sentences below the title.

Art (Magazine Pictures) and Theme

After you have finished reading a book or students have read one on their own, ask students to find and cut out magazine pictures and make a collage that seems to express the theme of the story. Students in small groups may explain to each other why their picture shows the theme of the book read. Younger students can create collages with language experience strips across the bottom that explain their themes. They can tape record their themes and why their picture shows the theme, or hold up their pictures and tell why the themes are shown in the pictures.

Student Stories and Themes

Students may write the title and theme of each of their stories on a ribbon that can wind around the room.

Theme Quilt

Students can create quilts, using geometric shapes (circles, squares, diamonds, or triangles) that appear in objects seen in the story. Students may use colors that appear in the story and write short quotes from different scenes on the quilt to show the theme. Geometric shapes can be in the center and on the border of the quilt. Quotes make up the main part of the quilt.

Theme Time Line

Students can create time lines, either as individuals or in small groups, to show how the theme shows up on the time line of the story.

Art (Cartoons) and Theme

Have students bring in cartoon strips that have the same themes as book themes or provide them for use in small discussion groups. Transparencies used with an overhead projector would work well here with young children. Some themes for students to hunt for in cartoons or comics include facing losses, coping with fears, friendship, courage, love, family relationships, and growing up.

Book Illustrations and Theme

Using a picture storybook, have students determine in a discussion, either in large groups or small, how the illustrations of a book show the theme.

Assessment: Theme Chart

Students can make this chart. They place the class definition of theme at the top of the chart and then choose one character from a book and write an example in which the character demonstrates the theme of the story. Post the chart, allowing each student a spot to write a title, character, and theme.

CHAPTER 8

The Big Picture: Style

TONE AND VOICE COME TOGETHER UNDER STYLE

The act of writing is an act of many choices. Too often, beginning writers seem to think that writing is an irrational accident. They have this feeling here [hand on heart] and they want to get it there [gesture of pouring toward paper]. And, if they get anything down on paper, they think it's got to be good because it's their own invention. Instead, the choices made in writing should be understood as conscious and deliberate acts. That way, style—through the experience of writing—will become unconscious again.[1]

Young writers need to practice the craft of writing and learn to make choices so that they can develop their style of writing. Just as painters who are learning how to paint must master basic techniques and then go on to develop their own way or "style of painting," young writers too must make "conscious and deliberate" acts of writing and write much and often. Young writers can develop their own style, which can become quite "unconscious" as they become expert writers, with a style that conveys their own voice and manner of writing.

WRITERS NEED TO DEVELOP THEIR OWN VOICE

In chapter 6, tone was described as one of the elements that a writer needs to think about when telling any story. Tone is part of a writer's style and part of the author's overall voice expressed in the story. Some authors, such as Walter Dean Myers, are able to write in a narrative "voice" that is humorous, as in *Won't Know Until I Get There*, slapstick, as in the Smiffy Blue mystery stories, or serious, as in his young adult novel, *Darnell Rock Reporting*.

Each author, though, has a unique style that is his or her own, such that he or she learns to recognize and hear that "voice" as if he or she were the reader listening in. While style may be seen as distinctive and identifiable by looking at many books by the same author, it is an elusive element. Walter Lorraine, who works as an editor for writers such as Allen Say and Lois Lowry, spoke in an interview with me about Lois Lowry's style:

> I loved *Number the Stars*. Lois has a natural inner ear for her story and the sound of her story. She is visual too, and at one time did professional photography. Again, the meter, the sound and the rhythm of the words are phenomenal. When you read books, you can judge them by how long it takes to get used to the style of the author. For many authors, it takes maybe half a chapter to get used to the writing. For Lois Lowry, it is one sentence, and you're comfortable with her. [2]

The author's "voice," demonstrated through style, includes tone and the other literary elements of character, setting, plot, and point of view. Joseph Bruchac talks about his own voice in his stories:

> Question: "As a storyteller, do you change traditional stories when they go into print? If so, could you give one example of how a part of a story changed as it went into print? Or if they don't change, why are they exactly the way you tell or have told them?"
>
> Joseph Bruchac: "When I retell traditional stories, I tell them in my own voice. That means that the words I choose, the descriptions of things, even some of the dialogue in them, come from the way I see that story in my mind. I may also add details which are true to the particular culture the story comes from, such as describing the appearance of an Iroquois elm bark longhouse with the smoke hole in the roof, when I tell the Mohawk story of 'The Brave Woman and the Flying Head.' My 'changes' may also be a result of the process of translation when I end up telling a differing version of a story that is fairly well known in English because I am retranslating it, looking at how it originally was told in, for example, Abenaki, and choosing different words than previous writers of that story chose. For example, the words *Ktsi Nwaskw* have been trans-

lated by some earlier writers as 'God.' I translate them more literally as 'Great Mystery.' However, I don't change the basics of the story. The major elements remain the same."[3]

The "voice" of the author is an element of style. But to write, as Joseph Bruchac does so well, an author needs to adapt/adopt many voices inside the stories themselves. Charlie Brashear, professor emeritus from San Diego State University, who has taught creative writing for over thirty years, says that "writers need to be able to write in many voices to fit each of the characters in their stories."[4]

As young writers learn to tell stories, they need to be able to create different voices for different characters in different situations with the appropriate tone. Those voices of character are not the overall voice of the writer, but part of it—showing characters with different traits and different patterns of action in a story.

STYLE: THE UMBRELLA

If we can think of "synergy" as the sum being greater than the parts, style would be that umbrella that includes tone, voice, and other literary elements—the tools of the craft of the writer that make writing bigger than life, more real than life, with everything held together for the benefit of story.

HELPING YOUNG WRITERS DEVELOP THEIR OWN STYLE

You can teach students how to work on their own style as writers. Young writers need to increase the time that they spend writing to be successful at writing fiction. They need practice. They also need to understand how to use language in order to develop a style of their own, paying attention to their own voices that they hear in their minds to be able to express them in their writing. They can then communicate their own particular voice as author and depict the voices of character in writing to the readers who make up their audience.

Readers hear story through this particular "authorial voice," enough so that they accept the voice telling the story and believe what is happening.

In that acceptance, they go with the writer, experiencing the total style of the author. To explain voice to students, you could talk about how thoughts appear in your mind, give examples of your own thoughts, and show students how those thoughts are the beginning of voice. Young writers need to know that all of us talk to ourselves and that "talking" in the voice we know can become our writing "voice" as well.

If students are not aware that they have a voice inside their heads that takes what their perceptions, senses, and feelings are and turns them into thoughts and then spoken phrases or sentences, then it is important to use further explanations with them. That they can hear their own voices means that they can use that sense of who they are, what they are thinking, and the way they are thinking to create stories peopled with real characters, who speak in believable voices.

MAKING CONSCIOUS CHOICES ABOUT WORD USE

Style includes choices that the writer makes for the following:

- Vocabulary and word choice
- Use of senses and imagery
- Figurative or particular language to express ideas
- Grammar and word order

Vocabulary and Word Choice

Vocabulary is an important part of style. Increasing students' awareness of how authors choose words to fit their audience will help students understand that choosing the right words makes a difference. To make that difference, young writers need to expand their vocabularies to have choices when they write. That is not to say that students should talk in abstractions or five-syllable formal words, but rather that they should be able to see how and why authors use the words and then delight in the infinite possibility for their own use of language.

Question: "What advice could you give young writers to encourage them to write?"

Eric Kimmel: "The best way to become a good writer is to become a good reader. You can't be a good writer unless you know what good writing is, and it's seldom the popular books that everyone else is reading. Read the best, most challenging books. They will build your vocabulary, show you new ways of creating characters and scenes. Ask yourself the question, why does one book or author keep you turning the pages while another book or author leaves you cold? What makes one book memorable and another forgettable? Above all, good writing is rewriting. All my books are written and rewritten many, many times. The biggest mistake most beginning writers make is they want their work to be perfect the first time they write it. It seldom happens. Read it over to yourself. Think about what you like about the story and what you don't like. What can be improved and how? What is unnecessary and can be cut. Then write it again. And again. And again. Do three serious rewrites of any story you write and you'll be surprised what a good writer you'll turn out to be. It's that simple! What you put in is what you get out."[5]

Eric Kimmel's questions above could become clear focus questions to ask students about their own reading and writing:

- What do you like about your story?
- What don't you like about your story?
- What can be improved?
- How can it be improved?
- What is unnecessary and can be cut out?

The choice of words, even from making decisions about using active verbs rather than passive verbs, is paramount to clear and expressive writing.

Use of Senses and Imagery

The use of the senses and imagery gives young writers a way to more clearly connect with readers. Seeing (such things as colors), hearing (sounds, emotion, tone), smelling (fragrances, odors), touching (nonverbal communication), and tasting (sweet, bitter, sour, cold, cool, hot, warm) place readers in the scenes they create in stories. A short section from Margarita González-Jensen's *The Butterfly Pyramid* works well to show the senses and tone of the characters toward the butterflies that have appeared around them. There is a sense of voice, tone, and style:

> He remembered Chilaam's word—magnificent! Now he knew the happiness the people had felt in the past. He wanted to cry out with joy, but he didn't dare for fear of scaring away the friendly butterflies. Slowly, he turned toward his mother, and saw that she, too, was covered with gently floating colors. They looked at each other, smiling and laughing and trying not to move.[6]

Sight, sound, and touch all combine to help us perceive this story in such a way that we are right there with the characters in the experience. Because the use of specific imagery and words that connote and denote the senses is so important in writing fiction, I have included books and activities that you may use to show how different writers use specific senses in their books. Some of the senses are major traits of character, essential to the plot, as in John Steptoe's *The Story of Jumping Mouse* or Joseph Bruchac's *The First Strawberries: A Cherokee Story*.

Figurative Language

The word *colors*, part of the figurative language of *The Butterfly Pyramid*, becomes a fine metaphor, standing for what the butterflies looked like—colors floating in the air, losing shape because of the sheer number of them. In the following section, some of the activities focus on the use of colors in idioms in English to give students a way to try out the use of colors in stories.

Similes and Metaphors. Even though the term *metaphor* is a concept for students in the upper grades, beyond the literal into the figurative, younger students need to become familiar with seeing them, hearing them, and writing their own. Younger students can recognize similes more easily in story text than they can recognize metaphors because they can hunt for the words *like* or *as*, which connect the images. For example, in the sentence "The clouds were like wild horses galloping across the sky," the word *like* tells us a comparison is being made. In the sentence "The clouds were wild horses galloping across the sky," the image is a direct one, with the clouds and horses standing in the place of one another in our mind. To understand and use metaphors is an important part of developing style when writing.

Some of the activities use idioms, the common metaphorical phrases in English, such as "as good as gold." These activities offer practice in understanding common images, so that writers can move from those images to creating their own and develop this part of style.

Choosing the Right Word. Part of any style are the words an author chooses to use. And, in choosing words for their precise meaning, authors distinguish between words that have similar meanings. For example, how does a writer choose between "hollered" and "yelled," or "giggled" and "laughed"? Which is better? Neither; but one word may be the better word to show something more clearly, or more appropriately in a particular story.

Have a Thesaurus on Hand. Verbs or adjectives may set the tone of a student's story. Writers use a thesaurus for writing, finding that right word for the right tone. Having a thesaurus in your class or on computer programs is a necessary part of your class reference tools for young writers.

The Use of Other Languages or Dialect in Fiction Writing. Writers may choose to use words from another language or dialect to tell the story and make it more authentic. How do writers determine what aspects of language or dialect to use for the "realism" of the story?

Eric Kimmel: "Language and dialect are two different things when it comes to writing. Remember that when you tell a story from another country, the characters are not speaking with an accent. They're speaking their own language perfectly and naturally. The best way to render this into English is to write and speak in your own natural language. In other words, if I were reading a story from Grimm's Fairy Tales, I wouldn't attempt to sound like Arnold Schwarzenegger. Nor, if I were writing the story, would I attempt to turn 'w's' into 'v's.' 'Look, Gretel!' Hansel said, 'It's der vicket vitch.' Attempting to read stories in dialect or with an accent seldom works, unless the reader knows the culture well or is particularly skilled. I always cringe when someone tells me they read *Hershel and the Hanukkah Goblins* with a 'Jewish' accent (whatever that is). I don't attempt to sound African when I read *Anansi*, or like Cheech Marin when I read a story from Mexico. Read it the way you speak. Children will understand the story, which is all they really care about. However, when writing a story, there are turns of phrase unique to regions and cultures. I visit Texas several times a year. Turns of phrase, images, descriptions used in Texas and the Southeast are extremely rich and colorful. Shorty Long isn't just dead; he's 'deader than a Christmas tree in August.' I listen for these, write them down, and think about how I can use them in the stories I write. Nobody reads my cowboy stories [*Charlie Drives the Stage; Four Dollars and Fifty Cents; Grizz!*] better than people from Texas and Oklahoma. They've got it down."[7]

In Gary Soto's books, page after page rings with Spanish words and phrases that add reality and cultural connections to his stories. For young writers, whose first language may be not English, showing them a way to choose words from another language to add to their stories will reinforce cultural connections and make their stories more authentic. For example, in Gary Soto's *The Cat's Meow*, a contemporary fiction story with fantasy elements, a cat speaks Spanish and then French. *The Cat's Meow* has the Spanish in the text of the story with footnotes for the translations. In Soto's more recent books, the Spanish is in the text with no footnotes to pull the eye away from the story. All of his stories read well, and the addition of Spanish authenticates the story.

> In order to write in dialect, you have to have a good ear. And if you can't hear how other people speak, then I suggest that you write how you sound. Remember, the reader will pick up immediately a false voice and judge the writer a fake.[8]

Grammar and Word Order

Grammar, which includes sentence structure, is part of style. Sentence structure varies with each writer. Some writers write in short sentences; some in long sentences. Word order is also an element of style. Some writers use standard subject-verb sentence structure; some may reverse the order and have the subjects at the end. Some writers use what we would consider nonstandard grammar in dialogue and description. If it is appropriate for the story written, young writers need to have the freedom to try out a variety of grammatical techniques.

WHAT DOES GOOD WRITING DO?

Authors, such as Laurence Yep, can give information to young writers to help them understand what good writing does: "Write about what you know. Good writing brings out the specialness of ordinary things [e.g., 'Imp' or 'Paintbrush']."[9] *The Imp That Ate My Homework* and *The Magic Paintbrush* include two ordinary things that are made extraordinary—the imp and the paintbrush. If young writers can learn to see things differently and create their stories from what they see, they will be well on their way to becoming fiction writers.

WHAT'S SO HARD ABOUT WRITING?

Writers will have parts of the process that are difficult for them. For some writers, it may be beginnings. Katherine Paterson, winner of the Hans Christian Anderson Award, speaks about that part of the process in an interview:

> Question from Sonya Haskins: "What's the most difficult aspect of writing for you?"
>
> Katherine Paterson: "I have a terrible time beginning. I have trouble coming up with the whole complex of ideas that you need to start a novel. Just getting started on a new book is always the hardest part for me. To overcome that, sometimes you just have to wait."[10]

The last quality of any human activity that can determine whether or not young writers may be successful in what they produce is whether or not they can stay with the task of writing over time. Allen Say, with a distinguished career as a writer and illustrator of children's literature, gives the perfect directive to young writers: "Persevere."[11]

STRATEGIES FOR HELPING WITH STYLE

Below are activities that will help your students with devices of style.

Journal Activity

Examining the Style of Authors. Students may have one section of their journals for "Style." Under that label, have students write the author's name then the title. Give students the following directions: "In your journal, write down one sentence or passage that you particularly liked from a story you've read. Place the sentence or passage in your journal with quotation marks before and after it. Why do you like this passage? Include one of the following: the choice of words (vocabulary), the use of images or the senses, similes or metaphors to express ideas, or another reason in your answer."

Comparing Styles of Authors. This activity makes style comparisons using similar subjects/selections from different works. Following are questions to ask students for written responses or for small-group discussions:

- How does each author tell you about description or action taking place?
- What are some of the word choices the author makes that you liked?
- Why did you like them?
- What feelings did each author show?
- Which author uses shorter sentences? Which author uses longer ones?
- Do any of the authors vary the word order? Where are the "subjects" or characters' names found?
- What are the verbs or action words in the story? Why do you think the author chose these words?
- What images does each author use?

Listed below are some possible books to use.

The Three Little Pigs: Ada, Alma Flor. *Dear Peter Rabbit*; Laird, Donivee Martin. *The Three Little Hawaiian Pigs and the Magic Shark*; Marshall, James. *The Three Little Pigs*; Scieszka, Jon. *The True Story of the 3 Little Pigs*

Cats: Say, Allen. *Allison*; Soto, Gary. *Chato's Kitchen*; Soto, Gary. *Summer on Wheels*; Soto, Gary. *Boys at Work*; Soto, Gary. *The Cat's Meow*

Journeys or Trips: Curtis, Christopher Paul. *Bud, Not Buddy*; Kimmel, Eric. *Onions and Garlic: An Old Tale*; Paterson, Katherine. *Celia and the Sweet, Sweet Water*; Paterson, Katherine. *Park's Quest*; Say, Allen. *Grandfather's Journey*; Soto, Gary. *Summer on Wheels* (see also chapter 7 for book titles)

Survival in Times of Political Strife: Lowry, Lois. *Number the Stars*; Orlev, Uri. *Island on Bird Street*; Paterson, Katherine. *Of Nightingales That Weep*; Taylor, Mildred D. *Roll of Thunder, Hear My Cry*; Uchida, Yoshiko. *Jar of Dreams*; Vos, Ida. *The Key Is Lost* (see also chapter 7 for book titles)

Adoption, Missing Parents, and Needing to Belong: Say, Allen. *Allison*; Curtis, Cristopher Paul. *Bud, Not Buddy*; Paterson, Katherine. *The Great Gilly Hopkins*; Myers, Walter Dean. *Me, Mop, and the Moondance Kid*; Myers, Walter Dean. *Won't Know Until I Get There*.

Losing Possessions: Soto, Gary. *Too Many Tamales*; Soto, Gary. *The Skirt*; Soto, Gary. "Barbie," in *Baseball in April and Other Stories*; Uchida, Yoshiko. *The Bracelet*

Seeing from the Other Side

Ask students to be a part of this activity with the following questions: "Pretend that you are the author of the book you have read. You are being interviewed for a talk show. How, when, where, and why did you write this book?"

Assessment: Sharpening Awareness of the Senses

With students, make a list of things in the classroom that you can see, touch, hear, smell, and taste. Post that list in the room.

Use picture books with primary and upper grades because well-written picture books supply rich imagery through visual details and story text. By using them for modeling, you can encourage students to use senses to create pictures in readers' minds. Have students list examples of different senses from the stories listed and then write their own sentences in a story that they are working on to show that particular sense. Picture storybooks and novels to use include:

Sight

> Ada, Alma Flor. *Mediopollito/Half-Chicken*.
> Bruchac, Joseph. *The First Strawberries: A Cherokee Story*.
> Goble, Paul. *Iktomi and the Buzzard*.
> Goble, Paul. *Iktomi Loses His Eyes*.
> González-Jensen, Margarita. *The Butterfly Pyramid*.
> Kimmel, Eric. *One Eyes, Two Eyes, Three Eyes: A Hutzul Tale*.
> Say, Allen. *Emma's Rug*.
> Taylor, Mildred D. *Let the Circle Be Unbroken* (novel).
> Yep, Laurence. *The Butterfly Boy*.

Sound

> Curtis, Christopher Paul. *Bud, Not Buddy* (novel).
> Goble, Paul. *Love Flute*.
> Hamilton, Virginia. *When Birds Could Talk and Bats Could Sing: The Adventures of Bruh Sparrow, Sis Wren, and Their Friends*.
> Medearis, Angela Shelf. *Dancing with the Indians*.
> Medearis, Angela Shelf. *Rum-a-Tum-Tum*.
> Medearis, Angela Shelf. *The Singing Man: Adapted from a West African Folktale*.
> Myers, Walter Dean. *The Blues of Flats Brown*.
> Paterson, Katherine. *The Wide Awake Princess*.
> Taylor, Mildred D. *Roll of Thunder, Hear My Cry* (novel).
> Taylor, Mildred D. *Song of the Trees* (novel).

Taste

> Bruchac, Joseph. *Ma'ii and Cousin Horned Toad*.
> Goble, Paul. *Iktomi and the Ducks*.
> *Goldilocks and the Three Bears* (any version).

Lester, Julius. *Sam and the Tigers: A New Telling of* Little Black Sambo.

Orlev, Uri. *The Island on Bird Street* (novel).

Soto, Gary. *Chato's Kitchen.*

Soto, Gary. *Too Many Tamales.*

Taylor, Mildred D. *The Well* (novel).

Smell

Nikly, Michelle. *The Perfume of Memory.*

Soto, Gary. *Chato's Kitchen.*

Steptoe, John. *The Story of Jumping Mouse: A Native American Legend.*

Uchida, Yoshiko. *The Bracelet.*

Touch

Castañeda, Omar. *Abuela's Weave.*

Duncan, Lois. *The Magic of Spider Woman.* Illustrated by Shonto Begay.

Goble, Paul. *Iktomi and the Boulder: A Plains Indian Story.*

Kimmel, Eric. *Seven at One Blow: A Tale from the Brothers Grimm.*

Kimmel, Eric. *The Tale of Aladdin and the Wonderful Lamp: A Story from* The Arabian Nights.

Young, Ed. *Seven Blind Mice.*

The Use of Colors

After you have read a story aloud, or students have read one on their own, you can strengthen student understanding of color by having them engage in a large-group discussion on what color means in a story or have them write what it means individually and then share their written answers in small groups. Finally, ask students why the use of colors is important in stories. Books (novels are marked as such) with colors in the titles include:

Ada, Alma Flor. *The Gold Coin*

Bruchac, Joseph. "White Weasel," in *Flying with the Eagle, Racing the Great Bear* (Abenaki tale).

Goble, Paul. *The Legend of the White Buffalo Woman*.

Hickox, Rebecca. *The Golden Sandal: A Middle Eastern Cinderella*.

Kimmel, Eric. *Count Silvernose: A Story from Italy*.

Myers, Walter Dean. *Shadow of the Red Moon* (novel).

Myers, Walter Dean. *Smiffy Blue, Ace Crime Detective: The Case of the Missing Ruby and Other Stories*.

Salisbury, Graham. *The Blue Skin of the Sea*.

Sneve, Virginia Driving Hawk. *Jimmy Yellow Hawk* (novel).

Taylor, Mildred D. *The Gold Cadillac* (novel).

Woodson, Jacqueline. *Maizon at Blue Hill* (novel).

Young, Ed. *Lon Po Po: A Red-Riding Hood Story from China*.

Young, Ed. *Red Thread*.

Colorful Expressions in Idiomatic Phrases

Idioms, in any language, add familiarity to what people say. Although they are trite when overused, idiomatic phrases can make dialogue or description sparkle if the author or writer creates a character who uses it in speech, making it a "trait" of the character. That use then makes a world more real and recognizable to the reader. The use of idioms can add to the style of the writer and the quality of the work. Idioms or parts of idioms could be titles for stories, such as "Water Under the Bridge," "Whatever Way the Wind Blows," or "The Silver Lining."

Below the activities are phrases/sentences that are idioms, with colors within them. Place some of the phrases/sentences on strips of paper. Pass them out to small groups of students.

Group Work on Idioms. 1. Ask students to read their phrase aloud. 2. Group members then figure out what the phrase means. (They may need to use a dictionary or thesaurus. Books or computer word processing programs will work here.) 3. Each group member comes up with a sentence for each of the phrases/sentences that is his or her own. 4. Group members share their sentences. 5. Group members discuss how this idiom might show up in a story and answer the following question: "When could you use this phrase in a story you have in mind?"

Application/Writing Practice. 1. Students write one sentence from one of the idioms used in the class that "fits" with a story that they have heard read aloud or read themselves. 2. While working on their own stories, students include one of the idiomatic phrases in dialogue or description or title of their work.

Samples of idiomatic expressions with "colors" to use with students include:

Blue: feeling blue, once in a blue moon, to have the blues, out of the blue

Gold: At the end of every rainbow is a pot of gold, as good as gold

Black: in the black, black as coal, black as jet, black as midnight, black and blue

Green: to give someone the green light, greenhorn, to have a green thumb, green with envy

Metallic: to have a golden touch, golden wedding anniversary, every cloud has a silver lining, silver-tongued

Red and pink: red as a lobster, seeing red, red-hot, in the pink, in the red

White: as white as snow

Yellow: yellow as a crow's foot

Other Idiomatic Expressions

Have students use idiomatic expressions from the list below in sentences to show that they understand what they mean. Ask them to explain what they mean. Then have them create very short stories that have the idiom within the story, either as a metaphor or as a real story happening. For example, "walking on eggs" might turn into a fantasy in which a character is really walking on eggs and the eggs are saying, "Don't tread on me."

Movement: walk on eggs

Time: go like clockwork

Moving water: go with the tide, swim upstream, fight the current

Day, night, and light: day in and day out, see daylight, day by day, fly by night, to see the light

Weather: under the weather, weather the storm, rain or shine, take by storm, shoot the breeze

Numbers in Stories

After reading one or several of the stories listed below, ask students to explain why numbers are important in the titles of these stories. Also ask students to write a story in which numbers are included in the title.

Ada, Alma Flor. *The Three Gold Oranges*.

Bruchac, Joseph. *Thirteen Moons on Turtle's Back*.

Goble, Paul. *Her Seven Brothers*.

Kimmel, Eric. *One Eyes, Two Eyes, Three Eyes: A Hutzul Tale*.

Kimmel, Eric. *Nanny Goat and the Seven Little Kids: Retold from the Brothers Grimm*.

Myers, Walter Dean. *The Story of the Three Kingdoms*.

Sneve, Virginia Driving Hawk. "The Twelve Moons," in *Grandpa Was a Cowboy and an Indian*.

Snyder, Dianne. *The Boy of the Three-Year Nap*. Illustrated by Allen Say.

Young, Ed. *Red Thread*.

Young, Ed. *Seven Blind Mice*.

Changing Descriptive Narration to Dialogue

Using a descriptive paragraph from a scene in a book, ask students to take the narrative and rewrite the paragraph with two characters talking, telling the reader what the scene is. Ask students the following questions: What did you have to do to make the change? How did the change from descriptive narration to dialogue change the scene?

Changing Dialogue to Descriptive Narration

Using a selection of dialogue from a scene in the book, have students take the dialogue and turn it into narrative description written in the third person. Ask students the following questions: What do you have to do to make the change? How is the passage/selection different from what it was originally?

Imitation of an Author's Style

Ask students to read several books by a favorite author. Have them write down what they can see that the author does with style. Refer to Journal Activity, "Comparing Styles of Authors." Then have them write paragraphs or short stories in the manner of their favorite author.

Compare two variants of the same story. "The White Buffalo Calf Woman," in Virginia Driving Hawk Sneve's *Grandpa Was a Cowboy and an Indian,* and Paul Goble's *The White Buffalo Calf Woman.* How does each author's style show a similar story? How is the treatment of the subject or theme the same? How is it different? Students may respond to questions orally in small-group discussions or in written form. Then they may write their own version of the story.

First and Last Pages

Find samples of first and last paragraphs of different stories that students have heard read aloud or read on their own. Have students compare the authors' different styles of beginning paragraphs, then their ending paragraphs. The following are some questions to ask students to complete orally in small groups or in writing activities:

- What makes each of the beginning paragraphs work well as beginnings to stories?
- What makes each of the ending paragraphs work well as story endings?

Comparison of Specific Content

Compare the way the journeys are shown and described in Alma Flor Ada's *Three Gold Oranges* in terms of sentence structure and description of events along the way with the journey taken in Gary Soto's *Summer on Wheels.* You could use this activity with any of the books listed in the Journal Activity in this chapter.

Literary Element Word Wall

Create a giant "Wall of Literary Elements" with the words in block letters under specific titles, using the following headings: Title, Character, Setting, Plot, Point of View, Theme, Examples of Style, and Tone. Over time, students can fill in each of these elements for a book that they have read.

Writing about Books

Have students write reviews of books for Internet companies at commercial and noncommercial locations. Have students write reviews of other classmates' stories and post them on a class computer site. A good question for classroom use is: "What advice could you give young writers to encourage them to write?"

> Joseph Bruchac: "Each of us sees the world in a unique way. When you write well, you tell your own story as no one else can tell it. Remember, if you don't tell your stories one of two things can happen. Either those stories will go untold, unshared, unheard or someone else will tell them and may tell them in a way that you will not find pleasing."[12]

CHAPTER 9

Assessment: Do Young Writers Know How to Write Fiction?

Young writers who master activities on literary elements from this book will gain an understanding of literary elements and ways to apply those elements to their own writing to create stories—original fiction.

Each of the chapters has strategies and assessment of the understanding of literary elements as well as strategies for the application of those elements to fiction writing. As you work with the strategies, you can align the goals and assessment of your writing workshop with the activities in this book. For example, if students are already keeping journals for a writing workshop, they could use those same journals for activities from this book.

MEETING OVERALL LITERACY GOALS

What is also important is to be able to see the "big picture" of literacy. Many of the strategies and assessments meet general literacy goals for grades K–6. The chart below gives an overview of how this book supports overall literacy goals that would be appropriate for students to have attained at the end of elementary school.

Overall Literacy Goals	Specific Knowledge and Activity from This Book
Identify in literary selections a sequence of events, which includes main ideas, facts, and supporting details.	Identify in narrative text of plot, kinds of plot, and problems/solutions for characters.
Identify elements of literature such as plot, character, setting tone, point of view, theme, and voice and style.	Use each element in a fictional writing activity.
Describe how diverse writers are influenced by their ethnic backgrounds and personal experiences.	Incorporate own background and personal experiences in creative writing assignments.
Describe in discussion or in a written assignment how diverse writers are or have been influenced by historical, social, or cultural events.	Having heard or read on one's own biographical and autobiographical information about diverse authors, make connections about the events and the writing of those events in fiction.
Demonstrate writing organizational skills for ideas, sentences, and paragraphs to create beginnings, middles, and ends.	Create a short story with beginning, middle, and end.
Use correct grammar in writing, including variety in sentence structure, correct capitalization, and correct punctuation.	Use "I" for first-person point of view, tag lines for speech, commas and quotation marks for speech.

Write in a different mode, such as narrative, to express ideas appropriate to a particular audience.	Create paragraphs, sketches, and short stories, in narrative mode for classroom and wider publication.
Be able to reflect on and evaluate one's own writing.	Use Writing Self-Assessment Notes (WSA Notes) for personal critiques, discussion with peers, conferencing with teachers.

KEEPING TRACK OF STUDENT WRITING

This system will enable you to keep track of student progress over time in your writers workshop. You could choose to use a variety of filing and long-term systems, including portfolios, to accumulate writings and assessments that show competency in the tools of the trade of creative writing. And because you may have a writers workshop that includes more than fiction writing in your literacy program, you will find references from a variety of sources on writers workshops for your use in the bibliography, under "Connections to Readers and Writers Workshops."

A management system of student work should be simple and easy for both teacher and students to use. A folder might be a simple portfolio system that has those items to be included printed on the inside of the front cover, so that students can check off what they place in the folder. Students could, of course, keep portfolios on a computer with the teacher having access for review of materials. However, some of the written work done in class would have to be scanned in for use by both you and students.

Students would have the responsibility to reflect on important items in the folders, such as a beginning work and an ending work. They could also evaluate their own progress in the understanding of each element, whether they feel that they have developed their own "voice" and how and why they believe this is so or not. They could comment on what they think is their best work, and why they think it is their best work. They could choose one story that they would change if they had more time, and say what they would change and how they would go about it.

AT A GLANCE

How students write what they write is important. You can use the following questions to ask graduate students who are teachers to share how they wrote papers, projects, poems, or short stories. This format would be easy for young writers to use. Using *At a Glance*, with its simple circling method, you can have students give you information about their writing, returned to you with the piece that they wrote.

How did you go about beginning your sketch, story, chapter? Circle one or more of the following: (a) Web cluster (b) Outline (c) Made a list of ideas (d) Talked with a classmate (e) Talked with my teacher (f) Wrote notes in my journal (g) I just wrote the sketch/story/chapter.

WSA 1: INFORMAL WRITING SELF-ASSESSMENT NOTES

As young writers learn to be perceptive of their own writing strengths and areas to develop, you can choose "Yes" and "No" formats for their responses. Students answer the following *Writing Self-Assessment 1 (WSA 1)* from questions on paper or on computer. They can keep these in their own files for future use or for you to use as appropriate checks of self-analysis of their writing. The first informal assessment are in a "Yes/No" format—questions that students can ask themselves.

Here are some questions to check on your story progress:

- Do I have one main character?
- Did I develop my character with one or more character traits?
- Did I say what my main character needs or wants?
- Is there somebody or something that works against my main character?
- Is there a tension or conflict between the main character and the antagonist that works against the main character?
- Did I have a time and place for my story?

- Did I write events in which the character tries to solve his or her problem?
- Did I use the senses in my story?
- Did I use colors or numbers in my story?
- Did I figure out how my main character would solve a problem?
- Did I show action in my story?
- Did the tension or conflict get resolved for my main character?
- Did I stay in the point of view that I chose?
- Did I stay in the tone that I started the story with?
- Did I vary my sentence structure so I have some long and some short sentences?
- Did I check my grammar, sentence structure, spelling, and punctuation?
- Did I figure out who the audience for my story will be?

WSA 2: FORMAL WRITING SELF-ASSESSMENT NOTES

Another assessment that will give you information on literary elements as well as how students express themselves about their own writing is more formal. A sample form is below.

Name
Title of Story

1. Who is the main character in the story?
2. What problem does he or she face?
3. Is there a character who works against your main character?
4. When and where does your story take place?
5. What is one event that takes place in the beginning of your story?
6. What is one event that takes place in the middle of your story?
7. What is one event that takes place in the end of your story?
8. Who is the audience for your story?
9. Did you use any of the senses in your story? If so, write one of the sentences in which you used sense imagery in your story.
10. Did you use any similes or metaphors? If you did, write one that you used.
11. Why did you choose the title you chose for your story?

WSA 3: WRITING SELF-ASSESSMENT NOTES ON THE WRITING PROCESS

The following questions allow students to focus on themselves as writers and are helpful for you to see how they work with the craft of fiction writing:

- What do you know about the writing process?
- What does a writer go through when he or she writes a story?
- What do you, as a writer, go through when you write a story?
- Write five sentences about things a writer does that are important to you as a writer.

Assessment references are available in the bibliography. Because young writers need to learn how to use the tools of fiction writing to become successful at short stories, chapter books, or later, novels, they will need much practice and time to write. An ongoing writers workshop in your classroom with extended time frames offers that possibility to students. As you use this book, I hope you discover how enjoyable the process of working with students on their writing can be.

Finally, successful fiction writers understand the craft of fiction writing and can tell stories—to entertain and enlighten readers. Young fiction writers can give their readers the powerful images that stay in the memory and imagination so that they and their readers can see eagles long, long after they are gone.

Selected Bibliography of Authors

VERNA AARDEMA

Borreguita and the Coyote. New York: Knopf, 1991.
Jackal's Flying Lesson: A Khoikhoi Tale. New York: Knopf, 1995.
Oh, Kojo! How Could You! An Ashanti Tale. New York: Dial, 1984.
Rabbit Makes a Monkey Out of Lion: A Swahili Tale. New York: Dial, 1989.
The Riddle of the Drum. New York: Four Winds Press, 1975.
Why Mosquitoes Buzz in People's Ears: A West African Tale. New York: Dial, 1975.

Autobiographical Resources

A Bookworm Who Hatched (Meet the Author). Katonah, N.Y.: Richard C. Owen Publishers, Inc., 1993.

ALMA FLOR ADA

Ada, Alma Flor, Wingeier-Rayo, Philip, Thorned, Janet. *Choices and Other Stories from the Caribbean*. Peoria, Ariz.: Friendship Press, 1993.
Daniel's Mystery Egg. New York: Harcourt Trade, 2000.
Dear Peter Rabbit. New York: Atheneum Books for Young Readers, 1994.
Friend Frog. New York: Harcourt, 2000.
El gallo que fue a la boda de su tío. New York: Penguin Putnam, 1998.
The Gold Coin. New York: Atheneum, 1991.
Jordi's Star. New York: G. P. Putnam's Sons, 1996.
The Lizard and the Sun / La lagartija y el sol. New York: Doubleday Books, 1997.

The Malachite Palace. New York: Atheneum Books, 1998.

Me llamo María Isabel. New York: Libros Colibrí, 1993.

Mediopollito: Half-Chicken: A New Version of a Traditional Story (R. Zubizarreta, trans.). New York: Doubleday, 1995.

La Moneda de oro (B. Randall, trans.). New York: Lectorum Publishers, 1996.

My Name Is María Isabel. New York: Atheneum Books for Young Readers, 1993.

Olmo and the Blue Butterfly. Beverly Hills, Calif.: Laredo, 1995.

Olmo y la Mariposa Azul (R. Zubizarreta, trans.). Beverly Hills, Calif.: Laredo Publishing Co., 1992.

El Papalote. Miami, Fla.: Santillana Publishing, 1992.

The Rooster Who Went to His Uncle's Wedding: A Latin American Folktale. New York: G. P. Putnam's Sons, 1992.

Serafina's Birthday. New York: Atheneum, 1992.

The Three Gold Oranges. New York: Atheneum, 1999.

The Unicorn of the West: El unicornio del oeste (R. Zubizarreta, trans.). New York: Atheneum, 1993.

Yours Truly, Goldilocks. New York: Atheneum Books, 1998.

Autobiographical Resources

Following is a list of books to use for insight into the storytelling ability of Alma Flor Ada. These books portray Alma Flor Ada's life in Cuba as a child and are written in first-person narration.

Under the Royal Palms: A Childhood in Cuba. New York: Atheneum Books for Young Readers, 1998. (Focus is on family and events that have shaped her life. Shows how each person has his or her own values, struggles, and dreams. This volume is a companion volume to *Where the Flame Trees Bloom*.)

Where the Flame Trees Bloom. New York: Atheneum, 1994.

Escribiendo desde el corazón / Writing from the Heart, a video published in Spanish- and English-language versions, *Meeting an Author* (video), and *Aprender cantando I y II* and *Como una flor* (cassettes).

SHONTO BEGAY

The books below are ones that Shonto Begay has written and illustrated. Others illustrated by Shonto Begay are listed under the following authors: Leigh Casler, Caron Lee Cohen, and Lois Duncan.

Navajo: Visions and Voices across the Mesa. New York: Scholastic, 1995.
Ma'ii and Cousin Horned Toad. New York: Scholastic, 1992.

JOSEPH BRUCHAC

The Arrow over the Door. New York: Penguin Putnam, 1998.
Between Earth and Sky: Legends of Native American Sacred Places. San Diego, Calif.: Harcourt Trade Publications, 1996.
Bowman's Store. New York: Penguin Putnam, 1997.
A Boy Called Slow: The True Story of Sitting Bull. New York: Penguin Putnam, 1995.
The Boy Who Lived with the Bears and Other Iroquois Stories. New York: HarperCollins, 1995.
Children of the Longhouse. New York: Penguin Putnam, 1996.
The Circle of Thanks. Mahwah, N.J.: BridgeWater Books, 1996.
Crazy Horse's Vision. New York: Lee & Low Books Inc., 2000.
Dawn Land. Golden, Colo.: Fulcrum Publishing, 1993.
Dog People. Golden, Colo.: Fulcrum Publishing, 1995.
Eagle Song. New York: Penguin Putnam, 1997.
The Earth under Sky Bear's Feet. New York: Penguin Putnam, 1995.
The First Strawberries: A Cherokee Story. New York: Penguin Putnam, 1993.
Flying with the Eagle, Racing the Great Bear: Stories from Native North America. Mahwah, N.J.: BridgeWater Books, 1997.
Four Ancestors. Mahwah, N.J.: BridgeWater Books, 1997.
Fox Song. New York: Penguin Putnam, 1993.
The Girl Who Married the Moon. Mahwah, N.J.: BridgeWater Books, 1996.
Gluskabe & the Four Wishes. New York: Penguin Putnam, 1995.
The Good Message of Handsome Lake. Oakland, Calif.: Unicorn Press Inc., 1979.
The Great Ball Game. New York: Penguin Putnam, 1994.
The Heart of a Chief. New York: Penguin Putnam, 1998.
How Chipmunk Got His Stripes. New York: Penguin Putnam, 2001.
Indian Mountain & Other Poems. Greenfield Center, N.Y.: Greenfield Review Literary Center, 1971.
Iroquois Stories: Heroes and Heroines, Monsters and Magic. Santa Cruz, Calif.: Crossing Press Inc., 1985.
Keepers of the Animals. Golden, Colo.: Fulcrum Publishing, 1991.
Keepers of the Earth. Golden, Colo.: Fulcrum Publishing, 1988.
Lasting Echoes. New York: Harcourt Trade Publishers, 1997.
Makiawisug. Uncasville, Conn.: Little People Publications, 1997.

The Man Who Loved Buffalo. New York: Harcourt Trade Publishers, 1998.
New Voices from the Longhouse. Greenfield Center, N.Y.: Greenfield Review
   Literary Center Inc., 1988.
The Next World. Santa Cruz, Calif.: Crossing Press Inc., 1978.
Pushing Up the Sky. New York: Penguin Putnam, 2000.
The Return of the Sun. Santa Cruz, Calif.: Crossing Press Inc., 1989.
Returning the Gift. Tucson: University of Arizona Press, 1994.
Roots of Survival. Golden, Colo.: Fulcrum Publishing, 1996.
Sacajawea. New York: Harcourt Trade Publishers, 2000.
Skeleton Man. New York: HarperCollins Children's Book Group, 1986.
Squanto's Journey. Austin, Tex.: Raintree Steck-Vaughn Publishers, 2000.
Stone Giants and Flying Heads: Adventure Stories of the Iroquois. Santa Cruz,
   Calif.: Crossing Press Inc., 1979.
The Story of the Milky Way: A Cherokee Tale. New York: Penguin Putnam, 1995.
Survival This Way. Tucson: University of Arizona Press, 1990.
Tell Me a Tale. New York: Harcourt Trade Publishers, 1997.
Thirteen Moons on Turtle's Back. New York: Penguin Putnam, 1992.
The Trail of Tears. New York: Random House Books for Young Readers, 1999.
Translator's Son. Merrick, N.Y.: Cross-Cultural Communications, 1980.
Turtle Meat & Other Stories. Duluth, Minn.: Holy Cow! Press, 1992.
"Turtle's Race with Bear," on the video *Animal Stories: Captivating Tales Tra-
   ditionally Told*. Atlas Video, 1991.
The Water's Between. Hanover, N.H.: University Press of New England, 1998.
When the Chenoo Howls. New York: Walker & Company, 1999.

Autobiographical Resources

Seeing the Circle. Katonah, N.Y.: Richard C. Owen Publishers, Inc., 1999.

DANIELLA CARMI

Samir and Yonatan (Yael Lotan, trans.). New York: Arthur A. Levine/Scholas-
   tic Press, 2000.

LEIGH CASLER

The Boy Who Dreamed of an Acorn. Illustrated by Shonto Begay. New York:
   Penguin Putnam, 1994.

OMAR CASTAÑEDA

Abuela's Weave. New York: Lee and Low, 1993.

SOOK NYUL CHOI

The Best Older Sister. New York: Bantam, Doubleday, Dell, 1997.
Halmoni and the Picnic. Boston, Mass.: Houghton Mifflin, 1993.
The Year of Impossible Goodbyes. Boston, Mass.: Houghton Mifflin, 1991.
Yunmi and Halmoni's Trip. Boston, Mass.: Houghton Mifflin, 1997.

CARON LEE COHEN

Cohen, Caron Lee, reteller. *The Mud Pony: A Traditional Skidi Pawnee Tale*.
    Illustrated by Shonto Begay. New York: Scholastic, 1988.

CHRISTOPHER PAUL CURTIS

Bud, Not Buddy. New York: Delacorte Press, 1999.
The Watsons Go to Birmingham—1963. New York: Delacorte Press, 1995.

LULU DELACRE

*De oro y esmeraldas: mitos, leyendas y cuentos populares de Latinoamerica
    (Golden Tales: Myths, Legends, and Folktales from Latin America)*. New
    York: Scholastic, 1996.
Nathan and Nicholas Alexander. New York: Scholastic, 1986.
Nathan's Balloon Adventure. New York: Scholastic, 1991.
Nathan's Fishing Trip. New York: Scholastic, 1988.
Peter Cottontail's Easter Book. New York: Scholastic, 1991.
Salsa Stories. New York: Scholastic, 2000.
Time for School, Nathan. New York: Scholastic, 1989.
Vejigante Masquerader. New York: Scholastic, 1993. (bilingual text)

DEMI

One Grain of Rice: A Mathematical Folktale. New York: Scholastic, 1997.

ROBERT DE SAN SOUCI

Cut from the Same Cloth. New York: Philomel, 1993.
The Talking Eggs: A Folktale from the American South (retold). New York: Dial Books for Young Readers, 1989.

LOIS DUNCAN

The Magic of Spider Woman. Illustrated by Shonto Begay. New York: Scholastic, 1996.

VALERIE FLOURNOY

The Patchwork Quilt. New York: Dial Press, 1985.

PAUL GOBLE

Adopted by the Eagles: A Plains Indian Story of Friendship and Treachery. New York: Simon and Schuster, 1994.
Beyond the Ridge. New York: Bradbury Press, 1989.
Brave Eagle's Account of the Fetterman Fight: 21 December 1866. Lincoln: University of Nebraska Press, 1992.
Crow Chief: A Plains Indian Story. New York: Orchard, 1992.
Death of the Iron Horse. New York: Bradbury, 1987.
Dream Wolf. New York: Simon and Schuster, 1990.
The Friendly Wolf. New York: Bradbury Press, 1974.
The Gift of the Sacred Dog: Story and Illustrations. New York: Simon and Schuster, 1980.
The Girl Who Loved Wild Horses: A Native American Tale. New York: Simon and Schuster, 1983.
The Great Race of the Birds and Animals. New York: Bradbury, 1985.
Her Seven Brothers. New York: Bradbury, 1988.
I Sing for the Animals. New York: Bradbury Press, 1991.
Iktomi and the Berries: A Plains Indian Story. New York: Orchard, 1992.
Iktomi and the Boulder: A Plains Indian Story. New York: Orchard, 1988.
Iktomi and the Buffalo Skull. New York: Orchard, 1991.

Iktomi and the Buzzard: A Plains Indian Story. New York: Orchard, 1994.
Iktomi and the Coyote: A Plains Indian Story. New York: Orchard, 1998.
The Legend of the White Buffalo Woman. New York: Simon and Schuster, 1984.
Love Flute. New York: Bradbury, 1992.

Autobiographical Resource

Hau Cola: Hello, Friend. Katonah, N.Y.: Richard C. Owen, 1994.

LUCIA M. GONZÁLEZ

The Bossy Gallito / El Gallo de bodas: A Traditional Cuban Tale. Illustrated by Lulu Delacre. New York: Scholastic, 1994.

MARGARITA GONZÁLEZ-JENSEN

Botas Negras. New York: Scholastic, 1993.
The Butterfly Pyramid. Bothell, Wash.: The Wright Group, 1997.

GEORGIA GUBACK

Luka's Quilt. New York: Greenwillow, 1994.

VIRGINIA HAMILTON

Drylongso. San Diego: Harcourt Brace Jovanovich, 1992.
The Girl Who Spun Gold. New York: Scholastic, 2000.
Her Stories: African American Folktales, Fairy Tales, and True Tales. New York: Scholastic, 1995.
The House of Dies Drear. New York: Macmillan, 1968.
In the Beginning: Creation Stories from Around the World. Econo-Clad Books, 1999.
The People Could Fly: American Black Folktales. New York: Knopf, 1985.

Plain City. New York: Scholastic, 1993.

The Planet of Junior Brown. New York: Simon & Schuster, 1971.

When Birds Could Talk and Bats Could Sing: The Adventures of Bruh Sparrow, Sis Wren, and Their Friends. New York: Scholastic, 1996

JOE HAYES

Little Gold Star / Estrellita de oro. A Cinderella Story. El Paso, Tex.: Cinco Puntos Press, 2000.

REBECCA HICKOX

The Golden Sandal: A Middle Eastern Cinderella Story. New York: Holiday House, 1998.

MINFONG HO

Brother Rabbit: A Cambodian Tale. New York: Lothrop, Lee & Shepard, 1997.

MARY HOFFMAN

Amazing Grace. New York: Dial Books for Young Readers, 1991.

Boundless Grace: Sequel to Amazing Grace. New York: Dial Books for Young Readers, 1995.

Starring Grace. New York: Dial Books for Young Readers, 2000.

COLBY HOL

The Birth of the Moon (Sibylle Kazeroid, trans.). North-South Books, 2000.

DEBORAH HOPKINSON

Sweet Clara and the Freedom Quilt. New York: Knopf, 1993.

BELINDA HURMENCE

Dixie in the Big Pasture. New York: Clarion, 1994.
A Girl Called Boy. New York: Houghton Mifflin, 1982.
The Night Walker. New York: Houghton Mifflin, 1988.
Tancy. New York: Houghton Mifflin, 1984. (young adult)
Tough Tiffany. New York: Doubleday, 1980.

ERIC KIMMEL

Anansi and the Magic Stick. New York: Holiday House, 2001.
Anansi and the Moss-Covered Rock. New York: Holiday House, 1988.
Anansi and the Talking Melon. New York: Holiday House, 1994.
Anansi Goes Fishing. New York: Holiday House, 1992.
Asher and the Capmakers: A Hanukkah Story. New York: Holiday House, 1993.
Baba Yaga. New York: Holiday House, 1991.
Bearhead. New York: Holiday House, 1991.
Bernal and Florinda: A Spanish Tale. New York: Holiday House, 1994.
Billy Lazroe and the King of the Sea: A Tale of the Northwest. Orlando, Fla.: Harcourt Brace & Company, 1996.
The Bird's Gift: A Ukranian Easter Story. New York: Holiday House, 1999.
Boots and His Brothers. New York: Holiday House, 1992.
The Chanukkah Guest. New York: Holiday House, 1990.
The Chanukkah Tree. New York: Holiday House, 1988.
Charlie Drives the Stage. New York: Holiday House, 1989.
A Cloak for the Moon: A Tale of Rabbi Nachman of Bratslav. New York: Holiday House, 2000.
Count Silvernose: A Story from Italy. New York: Holiday House, 1996.
Days of Awe: Stories for Rosh Hashanah and Yom Kippur. New York: Viking, 1992.
Four Dollars and Fifty Cents. New York: Holiday House.
The Four Gallant Sisters. New York: Henry Holt, 1992.
Gershon's Monster. New York: Scholastic, 2000.
The Ginger Bread Man. New York: Holiday House, 1993.
The Greatest of All: A Japanese Tale. New York: Holiday House, 1991.
Grizz. New York: Holiday House, 2000.
Hershel and the Hanukkah Goblins. New York: Holiday House, 1989.

I Know Not What, I Know Not Where. New York: Holiday House, 1994.

I Took My Frog to the Library. New York: Viking, 1990.

Iron John. New York: Holiday House, 1994.

The Jar of Fools: Eight Hanukkah Stories from Chelm. New York: Holiday House, 2000.

Montezuma and the Fall of the Aztecs. New York: Holiday House, 2000.

Nanny Goat and the Seven Little Kids: Retold from the Brothers Grimm. New York: Holiday House, 1990.

The Old Woman and Her Pig. New York: Holiday House 1992.

One Eye, Two Eyes, Three Eyes: A Hutzul Tale. Retold by Eric A. Kimmel. New York: Holiday House, 1996.

Onions and Garlic: An Old Tale. Retold by Eric A. Kimmel. New York: Holiday House, 1996.

Rimonah of the Flashing Sword: A North African Tale. New York: Holiday House, 1995.

Robin Hook, Pirate Hunter. New York: Scholastic, 2001.

The Rolling Stone and Other Read Aloud Stories. Houston, Tex.: Providence Publishing, 2000.

The Rooster's Antlers: A Story of the Chinese Zodiac. New York: Holiday House, 1999.

The Runaway Tortilla. New York: Winslow Press, 2000.

Seven at One Blow: A Tale from the Brothers Grimm. Retold by Eric A. Kimmel. New York: Holiday House, 1998.

Sirko and the Wolf: A Ukranian Tale. Adapted by Eric Kimmel. New York: Holiday House, 1997.

The Spotted Pony: A Collection of Hanukkah Stories. New York: Holiday House, 1992.

Sword of the Samurai. Lake Oswego, Oreg.: Browndeer Press, 1999.

The Tale of Aladdin and the Wonderful Lamp. New York: Holiday House, 1992.

The Tale of Ali Baba and the Forty Thieves. New York: Holiday House, 1996.

The Three Princes: A Tale from the Middle East. New York: Holiday House 1994.

Three Sacks of Truth. New York: Holiday House, 1993.

The Two Mountains: An Aztec Legend. New York: Holiday House, 2000.

The Valiant Red Rooster. New York: Henry Holt, 1995.

The Witch's Face. New York: Holiday House, 1993.

Website of the Cracked Cookies. New York: Dutton, 2001.

Website of the Warped Wizard. New York: Viking, 2001.

JULIUS LESTER

Ackamarackus: Julius Lester's Sumtuously Silly Fantastically Funny Fables.
New York: Scholastic, 2001.
Albidaro and the Mischievous Dream. Illustrated by Jerry Pinkney. New York:
Dial Press for Young Readers, 2000.
Further Tales of Uncle Remus. New York: Dial Press, 1990.
The Last Tales of Uncle Remus. New York: Dial Press, 1994.
More Tales of Uncle Remus. New York: Dial Press, 1988.
Sam and the Tigers: A New Telling of Little Black Sambo. New York: Dial
Books for Young Readers, 1996.
The Tales of Uncle Remus. New York: Dial Press, 1987.
What a Truly Cool World. New York: Scholastic, 1999.

AMY LITTLESUGAR

Freedom School, Yes! New York: Penguin Putnam, 2001.
Tree of Hope. New York: Philomel Books, 1999.

BETTY BAO LORD

In the Year of the Boar and Jackie Robinson. New York: HarperCollins, 1987.

RAFE MARTIN

The Rough-Face Girl. New York: Penguin Putnam, 1992.
The Shark God. New York: Scholastic, 2001.
The Storytelling Princess. New York: Penguin Putnam, 2001.

Autobiographical Resources

A Storyteller's Story. Katonah, N.Y.: Richard C. Owen, 1991.

CASEY A. MCGUIRE-TURCOTTE

How Honu the Turtle Got His Shell. New York: Raintree Publishers, Steck-
Vaughn, 1991.

LAWRENCE MCKAY

Journey Home. New York: Lee & Low, 1998.

PATRICIA C. MCKISSACK

The Dark Thirty: Southern Tales of the Supernatural. New York: Knopf, 1992. Random House, 1997.

Flossie and the Fox. New York: Dial Press, 1986.

A Million Fish . . . More or Less. New York: Alfred A. Knopf, 1992. Random House, 1996.

Mirandy and Brother Wind. Illustrated by Jerry Pinckney. New York: Knopf, 1988.

Run Away Home. New York: Scholastic, 1997.

Autobiographical Resources

Can You Imagine? Katonah N.Y.: Richard C. Owen, 1997.

ANGELA SHELF MEDEARIS

The Adventures of Sugar and Junior. New York: Holiday House, 1995.

Annie's Gifts. Orange, N.J.: Just Us Books, 1992.

The Boxcar Children: Mystery at the Alamo. Morton Grove, Ill.: Whitman, 1997.

The Boxcar Children: Mystery at the Fair. Illustrated by Charles Tang. Special #6. Morton Grove, Ill.: Whitman, 1996.

The Christmas Riddle. New York: Lodestar, 1993.

The Freedom Riddle. New York: E. P. Dutton, 1995.

The Ghost of Sifty-Sifty Sam. New York: Scholastic Press, 1997.

Haunts: Five Hair-Raising Tales. New York: Holiday House, 1996.

Nannie. New York: Atheneum Books for Young Readers, 1996.

Poppa's Itchy Christmas. New York: Holiday House, 1998.

Poppa's New Pants. New York: Holiday House, 1995.

Rum-a-Tum-Tum. New York: Holiday House, 1997.

Seven Spools of Thread: A Kwanzaa Story. Morton Grove, Ill.: Albert Whitman and Company, 2000.

Sharing Danny's Dad. Santa Monica, Calif.: Goodyear Publishing Company, 1995.

The Singing Man: Adapted from a West African Folktale. New York: Holiday House, 1994.

The Spray-Paint Mystery. New York: Little Apple, 1996.

Tailypo: A Newfangled Tale. New York: Holiday House, 1996.

Too Much Talk. Cambridge, Mass.: Candlewick Press, 1995.

What Did I Do to Deserve a Sister Like You? New York: Simon & Schuster, 1996.

WALTER DEAN MYERS

145th Street: Short Stories. New York: Delacourt Press, 2000.

At Her Majesty's Request: An African Princess in Victorian England. New York: Scholastic, 1999.

The Black Pearl and the Ghost, or One Mystery after Another. New York: Viking, 1980.

The Blues of Flats Brown. New York: Holiday House, 2000.

Darnell Rock Reporting. New York: Delacorte Press, 1994.

The Golden Serpent. New York: Viking, 1980.

How Mr. Monkey Saw the Whole World. New York: Delacorte Press, 1996.

The Legend of Tarik. New York: Scholastic, 1991.

Me, Mop, and the Moondance Kid. New York: Dell, 1990.

Mr. Monkey and the Gotcha Bird. New York: Delacorte, 1994.

Shadow of the Red Moon. New York: Scholastic, 1995.

Smiffy Blue, Ace Crime Detective: The Case of the Missing Ruby and Other Stories. New York: Scholastic, 1996.

Somewhere in the Darkness. New York: Scholastic, 1992.

The Story of the Three Kingdoms. New York: HarperCollins, 1995.

Tales of a Dead King. New York: Morrow, 1983.

Won't Know Until I Get There. New York: Viking Press, 1982.

MICHELLE NIKLY

The Perfume of Memory. Translated from the French. New York: Scholastic Press, 1999.

URI ORLEV

Lydia, Queen of Palestine. New York: Puffin Reprint, 1995.

The Island on Bird Street (Hillel Halkin, trans.). Boston, Mass.: Houghton Mifflin, 1984.

The Lady with the Hat (Hillel Halkin, trans.). Boston, Mass.: Houghton Mifflin, 1995.

The Man from the Other Side (Hillel Halkin, trans.). Boston, Mass.: Houghton Mifflin, 1991.

KATHERINE PATERSON

The Angel and the Donkey. Boston, Mass.: Houghton Mifflin, 1996.

Angels and Other Strangers: Family Christmas Stories. New York: HarperCollins, 1977.

The Bridge to Terabithia. New York: HarperCollins, 1978.

Celia and the Sweet, Sweet Water. Boston, Mass.: Houghton Mifflin, 1998.

Come Sing, Jimmy Jo. New York: Dutton, 1985.

The Field of Dogs. New York: HarperCollins, 2001.

Flip-Flop Girl. New York: Dutton, 1994.

The Great Gilly Hopkins. Santa Barbara, Calif.: ABC-Clio, 1978.

Jacob Have I Loved. Santa Barbara, Calif.: Cornerstone Books, 1990.

Jip: His Story. New York: Lodestar Books, 1996.

The King's Equal. New York: HarperCollins, 1992.

Marvin's Best Christmas Present Ever. HarperCollins Juvenile Books, 1997.

The Master Puppeteer. New York: Crowell, 1975.

A Night Clear: Stories for Christmas Season, 1998.

Of Nightingales That Weep. New York: Crowell, 1974.

Over the Water (with M. Casey). New York: Henry Holt, 1994.

Parks Quest. New York: Lodestar Books, 1988.

Parzival: The Quest of the Grail Knight (with W. Parzival). New York: Lodestar Books, 1998.

The Sign of Chrysanthemum. New York: Harper Trophy, 1988.

The Smallest Cow in the World. New York: HarperCollins, 1991.

The Tale of the Mandarin Ducks. New York: Lodestar Books, 1990.

The Wide Awake Princess. Boston, Mass.: Houghton Mifflin, 2000.

Autobiographical Resources

"Historical Fiction: Some Whys and Hows." *Booklist*, Vol. 95, No. 15 (April 1, 1999): p. 1430.

Part of Me Died, Too: Stories of Creative Survival Among Bereaved Children and Teenagers (with V. L. Fry). New York: Penguin Putnam, 1995.
The Spying Heart. New York: Lodestar Books, 1989.
When I Was Your Age: Original Stories about Growing Up (with A. Ehrlich and M. P. Osborne). Cambridge, Mass.: Candlewick Press, 1996.

PATRICIA POLACCO

Appelemando's Dream. New York: Penguin Putnam, 1999.
The Butterfly. New York: Penguin Putnam, 2000.
The Keeping Quilt. New York: Simon & Schuster, 1998.
Picnic at Mudsock Meadow. New York: Penguin Putnam, 1992.
Pink and Say. New York: Penguin Putnam, 1994.
Thundercake. New York: Penguin Putnam, 1997.
The Trees of the Dancing Goats. New York: Simon & Schuster, 1997.
Uncle Isaaco. New York: Philomel, 1997.

Autobiographical Resources

Firetalking. Katonah, N.Y.: Richard C. Owen, 1994.

GRAHAM SALISBURY

The Blue Skin of the Sea. New York: Delacorte, 1992.
Jungle Dogs. New York: Delacorte, 1998.
Under the Blood-Red Sun. New York: Delacorte, 1994.

ALLEN SAY

Allison. Boston, Mass.: Houghton Mifflin Co., 1997.
The Bicycle Man. Boston, Mass.: Houghton Mifflin Co., 1982.
El Chino. Boston, Mass.: Houghton Mifflin Co., 1990.
Emma's Rug. Boston, Mass.: Houghton Mifflin Co., 1996.
The Feast of Lanterns. New York: Harper & Row, 1976.
Grandfather's Journey. Boston, Mass.: Houghton Mifflin Co., 1993.
Home of the Brave. Boston, Mass.: Houghton Mifflin Co., 2002.
The Lost Lake. Boston, Mass.: Houghton Mifflin Co., 1989.

Once under the Cherry Blossom Tree: An Old Japanese Tale. New York: Harper & Row, 1974.
River Dream. Boston, Mass.: Houghton Mifflin Co., 1988.
The Sign Painter. Boston, Mass.: Houghton Mifflin Co., 2000.
Stranger in the Mirror. Boston, Mass.: Houghton Mifflin Co., 1995.
Tea with Milk. Boston, Mass.: Houghton Mifflin Co., 1999.
Tree of Cranes. Boston, Mass.: Houghton Mifflin Co., 1991.

Autobiographical Resources

The Inn-Keeper's Apprentice. New York: Harper & Row, 1979.
The Ink-Keeper's Apprentice: An Autobiographical Novel. Demco Media, 1996.

SHIVKUMAR

Stories from the Panchatantra. New Delhi: Children's Book Trust, 2000. First printed in 1979.

VIRGINIA DRIVING HAWK SNEVE

Betrayed. New York: Holiday House, 1974.
The Chichi Hoohoo Bogeyman. Lincoln: University of Nebraska Press, 1975. Reprinted in 1993 by arrangement with Virginia Driving Hawk Sneve and Holiday House.
Dancing Teepees: Poems of American Indian Youth. New York: Holiday House, 1989.
Enduring Wisdom: Sayings from American Indians. New York: Holiday House, 2000.
High Elk's Treasure. New York: Holiday House, 1972.
Jimmy Yellow Hawk. New York: Holiday House, 1972.
The Trickster and the Troll. Lincoln: University of Nebraska Press, 1997.
"The Twelve Moons," in *Grandpa Was a Cowboy and an Indian*. Lincoln: University of Nebraska Press, 2000.
When Thunders Spoke. New York: Holiday House, 1974.

About the Author

Completing the Circle. Lincoln: University of Nebraska Press, 1995.

DIANNE SNYDER

The Boy of the Three Year Nap. Illustrated by Allen Say. New York: Houghton Mifflin, 1988.

Siesta-De-Tres-Anos. Illustrated by Allen Say. Miami, Fla.: Santillana Publishing Co., 1995.

GARY SOTO

Baseball in April and Other Stories. Orlando, Fla.: Harcourt, 1990.

Big Bushy Mustache. New York: Knopf, 1998.

Boys at Work. New York: Bantam, 1995.

The Cat's Meow. New York: Scholastic Inc., by arrangement with Strawberry Hill Press, Portland, Ore., 1987.

Chato and the Party Animals. New York: G. P. Putnam's Sons, 2000.

Chato's Kitchen. New York: Putnam, 1995.

If the Shoe Fits. New York: G. P. Putnam's Sons, 2002.

Local News. San Diego, Calif.: Harcourt Brace, 1993.

Neighborhood Odes. New York: Harcourt, 1992. (This book of twenty-one poems reflects Soto's Latino heritage and could be used for brainstorming to consider culture and events that might lead to stories.)

Off and Running. New York: Delacorte Press, 1996.

The Old Man and the Door. New York: Putnam, 1996.

Pacific Crossing. San Diego, Calif.: Harcourt, 1992.

The Pool Party. New York: Delacorte Press, 1993.

The Skirt. New York: Delacorte Press, 1992.

Too Many Tamales. New York: G. P. Putnam's Sons, 1993.

Gary Soto Works for Older Students

The Effects of Knut Hamsun on a Fresno Boy: Recollections and Short Essays. New York: Persea Books, 2001.

A Fire in My Hands: A Book of Poems. Madison, Wisc.: Turtleback Books, 1990.

My Little Car. New York: Putnam, 2001.

Nerdlandia. New York: Putnam, 2000.

Nickel and Dime. Albuquerque: University of New Mexico Press, 2000.

Petty Crimes. New York: Harcourt, 1998.

Summer on Wheels. New York: Scholastic, 1995.
Taking Sides. San Diego, Calif.: Harcourt Brace Jovanovich, 1992.

JOHN STEPTOE

Daddy Is a Monster . . . Sometimes. New York: Lippincott, 1980.
Jeffrey Bear Cleans Up His Act. New York: Lothrop, 1983.
Mufaro's Beautiful Daughters: An African Tale. New York: Lothrop, 1987.
Stevie. New York: Harper, 1969.
The Story of Jumping Mouse: A Native American Legend. New York: Lothrop, 1984.
Uptown. New York: Harper, 1970.

ELEANORA E. TATE

A Blessing in Disguise. New York: Delacorte Press, 1995.
Don't Split the Pole: Tales of Down Home Wisdom. New York: Delacorte Press, 1997. (Seven stories on idioms)
Front Porch Stories at the One-Room School. New York: Bantam Books, 1992.
Just an Overnight Guest. New York: Penguin Putnam, 1980.
The Minstrel's Melody. Middleton, Wisc.: Pleasant Company Publications, 2001.
The Secret of Gumbo Grove. Danbury, Conn.: Franklin Watts, Inc., 1987.
Thank You, Dr. Martin Luther King. Danbury, Conn.: Franklin Watts, Inc., 1990.

MILDRED D. TAYLOR

The Friendship. New York: Dial Books for Young Readers, 1987.
The Gold Cadillac. New York: Dial Press, 1987.
The Land. New York: Dial Books, 2001.
Let the Circle Be Unbroken. New York: Dial Press, 1981.
Mississippi Bridge. New York: Dial Books for Young Readers, 1990.
The Road to Memphis. New York: Dial Books, 1990.
Roll of Thunder, Hear My Cry. New York: Dial Press, 1976.
Song of the Trees. New York: Dial Press, 1975.
Sprinting Backwards to God. New York: Scholastic, 1999.
The Well: David's Story. New York: Penguin Putnam, 1995.

Books about Mildred Taylor

Crowe, Chris. *Presenting Mildred Taylor*. New York: Macmillan Reference
  Library, 1999.

FRANCES TEMPLE

Grab Hands and Run. New York: Harper Trophy, 1995.
Tiger Soup: An Anansi Story from Jamaica. New York: Richard Jackson
  Book/Orchard, 1991.
Tonight, by Sea: A Novel. New York: A Richard Jackson Book/Orchard, l995.
  Harper Trophy, l996.

YOSHIKO UCHIDA

The Best Bad Thing. New York: Atheneum, 1983.
The Bracelet. New York: Philomel Books, 1993.
Dancing Kettle. Berkeley, Calif.: Creative Arts, 1986.
Jar of Dreams. New York: Atheneum, 1981.
Journey Home. New York: Atheneum, 1978.
Journey to Topaz. Berkeley, Calif.: Creative Arts, 1985.
Magic Listening Cap: More Folk Tales from Japan. New York: Harcourt
  Brace, 1955.
Magic Purse. New York: Margaret McElderry, 1993.
Picture Bride. Flagstaff, Ariz.: Northland Press, 1987.
Samurai of Gold Hill. New York: Scribners, 1972.
Sea of Gold and Other Tales from Japan. New York: Scribners, 1965.

Autobiographical Resources

Desert Exile. Seattle: University of Washington, 1982.
Invisible Thread. Engelwood, N.J.: Julian Messner, 1991.

IDA VOS

Dancing on the Bridge of Avignon. New York: Houghton Mifflin, 1995.
Hide and Seek. New York: Houghton Mifflin, 1991.
The Key Is Lost. (Terese Edelstein, trans.). New York: HarperCollins, 2000.

JACQUELINE WOODSON

Hush. New York: G. P. Putnam's Sons, 2002.
I Hadn't Meant to Tell You This. New York: Delacorte, 1992.
Last Summer with Maizon. New York: Delacorte, 1992.
Maizon at Blue Hill. New York: Delacorte, 1992.
Miracle's Boys. New York: Penguin Putnam, 2000.
The Other Side. New York: G. P. Putnam's Sons, 2001.

LAURENCE YEP

The Amah. New York: Putnam, 1999.
American Dragons: Twenty-Five Asian American Voices. New York: Harper-
    Collins, 1993.
Angelfish. New York: Putnam, 2001.
Bug Boy. New York: Hyperion Books, 2000.
The Butterfly Boy. New York: Farrar, Straus & Giroux, 1993.
The Case of the Firecrackers. New York: HarperCollins, 1999.
The Case of the Goblin Pearls. New York: HarperCollins, 1997.
The Case of the Lion Dance. New York: HarperCollins, 1998.
Child of the Owl. New York: HarperCollins, 1977.
Cockroach Cooties. New York: Hyperion Books, 2000.
The Cook's Family. New York: Putnam Publishing Group, 1998.
The Dragon Prince: A Chinese Beauty and the Beast Tale. New York: Harper-
    Collins, 1997.
Dragonwings. New York: Harper & Row, 1975.
Dream Soul. New York: HarperCollins, 2000.
The Ghost Fox. New York: Scholastic, 1994.
The Imp That Ate My Homework. New York: HarperCollins, 1998.
The Khan's Daughter. New York: Scholastic, 1997.
Later, Gator. New York: Hyperion Press, 1995.
The Magic Paintbrush. New York: HarperCollins, 2000.
The Rainbow People. New York: Harper & Row, 1989.
Ribbons. New York: Penguin Putnam, 1996.
The Star Fisher. New York: William Morrow & Co., 1991.
Tree of Dreams: Ten Tales from the Garden of Night. Mahwah, N.J.: Bridge-
    water Books, 1997.

Books about the Author

The Lost Garden. Magnolia, Mass.: Peter Smith Publisher, 1998.
Presenting Laurence Yep. United States Twayne Author Series, No. 256. New
  York: Macmillan Library Reference, 1995.

ED YOUNG

Donkey Trouble. New York: Alladin Paperbacks, 1998.
Lon Po Po: A Red-Riding Hood Story from China. New York: Penguin Putnam,
  1989.
The Lost Horse. San Diego, Calif.: Harcourt Brace, 1998.
Monkey King. New York: HarperCollins, 2001.
Mouse Match. San Diego, Calif.: Harcourt Brace, 1997.
Night Visitors. New York: Philomel, 1995.
Red Thread. New York: Philomel, 1993.
Seven Blind Mice. New York: Philomel, 1992.

Places of Birth and Birthdays for Authors

Use the following places and dates to construct maps of where authors were born and to celebrate their books during their birth months.

January

Alma Flor Ada	Camaguey, Cuba	January 3, 1938
Minfong Ho	Rangoon, Burma	January 7, 1951
Julius Lester	St. Louis, Missouri	January 27, 1939
Rafe Martin	New York	January 22, 1946

February

Shonto Begay	Near Shonto, Arizona	February 7, 1954
Deborah Hopkinson	Lowell, Massachusetts	February 4, 1952
Uri Orlev	Warsaw, Poland	February 24, 1931
Virginia Driving Hawk Sneve	Rosebud, Dakota (Sioux Tribe)	February 21, 1933
Jacqueline Woodson	Columbus, Ohio	February 12, 1964

March

Margarita González-Jensen	San Antonio, Texas	March 9, 1948
Virginia Hamilton	Yellow Springs, Ohio	March 12, 1936

| Amy Littlesugar | Bermuda | March 8, 1953 |
| Lois Lowry | Honolulu, Hawaii | March 20, 1937 |

April

Lois Duncan	Philadelphia, Pennsylvania	April 28, 1934
Valerie Flournoy	Camden, New Jersey	April 17, 1952
Rebecca Hickox		April 1, 1949
Mary Hoffman	East Leigh, Hampshire, England	April 20, 1945
Graham Salisbury	Philadelphia, Pennsylvania	April 11, 1944
Gary Soto	Fresno, California	April 12, 1952
Eleanora E. Tate	Canton, Missouri	April 16, 1948

May

| Christopher Paul Curtis | Flint, Michigan | May 10, 1954 |

June

| Verna Aardema | New Era, Michigan | June 6, 1911 |
| Laurence Yep | San Francisco, California | June 14, 1948 |

July

| Patricia Polacco | Lansing, Michigan | July 11, 1944 |

August

Belinda Hurmence	Oklahoma	August 20, 1921
Lawrence McKay	Pittsburgh, Pennsylvania	August 24, 1948
Patricia C. McKissack	Nashville, Tennessee	August 2, 1944
Walter Dean Myers	Martinsburg, West Virginia	August 12, 1937

| Allen Say | Yokohama, Japan | August 28, 1937 |
| Frances Temple | Washington, D.C. | August 15, 1945 |

September

Omar Castañeda	Guatemala City, Guatemala	September 6, 1954
Demi	Cambridge, Massachusetts	September 2, 1942
Paul Goble	Surrey, England	September 17, 1933
Jon Scieszka	Flint, Michigan	September 8, 1954
John Steptoe	Brooklyn, New York	September 14, 1950
Mildred Taylor	Jackson, Mississippi	September 13, 1943

October

Joseph Bruchac	Saratoga Springs, New York	October 16, 1942
Eric Kimmel	Brooklyn, New York	October 30, 1946
Katherine Paterson	Qing Jiang, China	October 31, 1932
Robert D. San Souci	San Francisco, California	October 10, 1946

November

Joe Hayes	Ross Township, Pennsylvania	November 12, 1945
Betty Bao Lord	Shanghai, China	November 3, 1938
Angela Shelf Medearis	Hampton, Virginia	November 16, 1956
Yoshiko Uchida	Alameda, California	November 24, 1921
Ed Young	Tientsin, China	November 28, 1931

December

| Lulu Delacre | Rio Piedras, Puerto Rico | December 20, 1957 |
| Ida Vos | Groningen, Netherlands | December 13, 1931 |

Notes

PREFACE

1. Artistic statement for his paintings and prints. Reprinted with permission from Shonto Begay.
2. Reprinted from *Something about the Author*, Anne Commire, editor, Vol. 58, p. 138.
3. Patricia Enciso, "Integrating 'Cultural Imagination'," *The Reading Teacher*, Vol. 47, No. 4 (December 1993/January 1994): pp. 336–337. Enciso clarifies the term further. "Cultural imagination," she says, "refers to our *capacity* to use the vivid montage of everyday images, languages, places and times to *inform our sense of identity*" (p. 336).
4. From *Flying with the Eagle*, *Racing the Great Bear* (Mahwah, N.J.: BridgeWater Books, 1997), p. x.
5. Margarita González-Jensen and Norma Sadler, "Behind Closed Doors: Status Quo Bias in Read Aloud Selections," *Equity and Excellence in Education*, Vol. 30, No. 1 (April 1997): pp. 27–31.
6. Norma Sadler, interview with Margarita González-Jensen, June 19, 2000.
7. Norma Sadler, interview with Alma Flor Ada, March 19, 2001.
8. Norma Sadler, interview with Margarita González-Jensen, June 19, 2000.
9. Norma Sadler, interview with Eric Kimmel, October 20, 2000.
10. Norma Sadler, interview with Margarita González-Jensen, June 19, 2000.

11. Norma Sadler, interview with Virginia Driving Hawk Sneve, September 9, 2000.
12. Norma Sadler, interview with Paul Goble, November 3, 2000.

CHAPTER ONE

1. Vicki Spandel, *Creating Writers through Six-Trait Writing Assessment and Instruction*. Third Edition. (Reading, Mass.: Longman, 2000).
2. Norma Sadler, interview with Margarita González-Jensen, June 19, 2000.
3. Norma Sadler, interview with Paul Goble, November 3, 2000.
4. Marie Dionesio, "Responding to Literary Elements through Mini-lessons and Dialogue Journals," *English Journal*, Vol. 80, No. 1 (1991): pp. 40–44.
5. Norma Sadler, interview with Laurence Yep, October 26, 2000.
6. Norma Sadler, interview with Walter Dean Myers, November 26, 2000.
7. David Weich Interview with Christopher Paul Curtis, April 5, 2000.

CHAPTER TWO

1. Norma Sadler, interview with Eric Kimmel, October 20, 2000.
2. Martha Davis Beck, "Allen Say: Interview," *Riverbank Review* (Fall 1999): pp. 22–25.
3. Norma Sadler, interview with Joseph Bruchac, October 17, 2000.
4. Norma Sadler, interview with Virginia Driving Hawk Sneve, September 9, 2000.
5. Norma Sadler, interview with Margarita González-Jensen, June 19, 2000.
6. Norma Sadler, interview with Walter Dean Myers, November 26, 2000.
7. Norma Sadler, interview with Eric Kimmel, October 20, 2000.
8. Norma Sadler, interview with Gary Soto, October 5, 2000.
9. From *High Elk's Treasure* (New York: Holiday House, 1972), p. 25. Reprinted with permission from Virginia Driving Hawk Sneve.

10. Norma Sadler, interview with Margarita González-Jensen, June 19, 2000.
11. Norma Sadler, interview with Shonto Begay, March 6, 2001.
12. Norma Sadler, interview with Eric Kimmel, October 20, 2000.

CHAPTER THREE

1. From *Anansi Goes Fishing* (New York: Holiday House, 1992).
2. Norma Sadler, interview with Eric Kimmel, October 20, 2000.
3. Norma Sadler, interview with Paul Goble, November 3, 2000.
4. From Allen Say's Caldecott Medal Acceptance Speech as it appeared in *The Horn Book Magazine*, July 1994. Reprinted with permission from Allen Say.
5. From *Mississippi Bridge* (New York: Dial Books for Young Readers, 1990), p. 7.
6. From *The Fun House* (Burbank: Baymax Productions, 1991), p. 1.
7. Norma Sadler, interview with Margarita González-Jensen, June 19, 2000.
8. Martha Davis Beck, "Allen Say: Interview," *Riverbank Review* (Fall 1999): pp. 22–25.

CHAPTER FOUR

1. Norma Sadler, interview with Walter Dean Myers, November 26, 2000.
2. Norma Sadler, interview with Joseph Bruchac, October 17, 2000.
3. Norma Sadler, interview with Virginia Driving Hawk Sneve, September 9, 2000.
4. Norma Sadler, interview with Virginia Driving Hawk Sneve, September 9, 2000.
5. From *Jimmy Yellow Hawk* (New York: Holiday House, Inc., 1972).
6. From Eric Kimmel's *Hershel and the Hannukah Goblins* (New York: Holiday House, 1985), p. 1.
7. Norma Sadler, interview with Gary Soto, October 5, 2000.
8. Norma Sadler, interview with Walter Dean Myers, November 26, 2000.

CHAPTER FIVE

1. Norma Sadler, interview with Walter Dean Myers, November 26, 2000.
2. From the Mildred D. Taylor Penguin Putnam Catalog Biography, copyright © 2000 by Penguin Putnam Books for Young Readers. Used by permission of Penguin Putnam Books for Young Readers, a division of Penguin Putnam, Inc.
3. Norma Sadler, interview with Gary Soto, October 5, 2000.
4. Norma Sadler, interview with Virginia Driving Hawk Sneve, September 9, 2000.
5. From *My Name Is María Isabel* (New York: Atheneum, 1993), p. 12.
6. Norma Sadler, interview with Alma Flor Ada, March 19, 2001.
7. Norma Sadler, interview with Joseph Bruchac, October 17, 2000.
8. Norma Sadler, interview with Paul Goble, November 3, 2000.
9. From *The Rooster Who Went to His Uncle's Wedding* (New York: Penguin Putnam, 1993).
10. Norma Sadler, conversations with Alma Flor Ada.

CHAPTER SIX

1. Martha Davis Beck, "Allen Say: Interview," *Riverbank Review* (Fall 1999): pp. 22–25.
2. From *The First Strawberries: A Cherokee Story* (New York: Penguin Putnam, 1993).
3. Norma Sadler, interview with Laurence Yep, October 26, 2000.
4. Norma Sadler, interview with Laurence Yep, October 26, 2000.

CHAPTER SEVEN

1. Norma Sadler, interview with Joseph Bruchac, October 17, 2000.
2. Norma Sadler, interview with Virginia Driving Hawk Sneve, September 9, 2000.
3. Norma Sadler, interview with Shonto Begay, February 26, 2001.

4. From *Something about the Author*, vol. 58, p. 138. Reprinted with permission from Gayle Research Inc.
5. From Allen Say's Caldecott Medal Acceptance Speech. Reprinted with permission from Allen Say.

CHAPTER EIGHT

1. Norma Sadler, interview with Charles Brashear, June 25, 2001.
2. Norma Sadler, "Interview with Walter Lorraine." As it appeared in *Portals*, Vol. 1, No. 2 (Spring 1994): p. 22. Reprinted with permission from Norma Sadler.
3. Norma Sadler, interview with Joseph Bruchac, October 17, 2000.
4. Norma Sadler, interview with Charles Brashear, June 25, 2001.
5. Norma Sadler, interview with Eric A. Kimmel, October 22, 2000.
6. *The Butterfly Pyramid* (Bothel, Wash.: The Wright Group, 1997), p. 22.
7. Norma Sadler, interview with Eric A. Kimmel, October 22, 2000.
8. Norma Sadler, interview with Gary Soto, October 5, 2000.
9. Norma Sadler, interview with Laurence Yep, October 26, 2000.
10. Sonya Haskins, "Five Questions: Katherine Paterson," *Writers Digest* (July 2000): p.8. Reprinted with permission from Sonya Haskins.
11. Norma Sadler, interview with Allen Say, October 16, 2000.
12. Norma Sadler, interview with Joseph Bruchac, October 27, 2000.

Bibliography

CONNECTIONS TO READERS AND WRITERS WORKSHOPS

Aregiado, Nancy, and Mary Dill. *Let's Write: A Practical Guide to Teaching Writing in the Early Grades*. New York: Scholastic, 1998.

Atwell, Nancy. *In the Middle: New Understandings about Writing, Reading, and Learning*. Second Edition. Portsmouth, N.H.: Heinemann, 1998.

Avery, Carol. . . . *And with a Light Touch*. Westport, Conn.: Heinemann, 1993.

Barton, Bob. *Telling Stories Your Way: Storytelling and Reading Aloud in the Classroom*. York, M.E.: Stenhouse Publishers, 2000.

Bauer, Marion Dane. *What's Your Story: A Young Person's Guide to Writing Fiction*. New York: Clarion, 1992.

Beaver, Teri. *The Author's Profile: Assessing Writing in Context*. York, M.E.: Stenhouse Publishers, 1998.

Blair, Heather A. "They Left Their Genderprints: The Voice of Girls in Text." *Language Arts,* Vol. 75, No. 1 (January 1998): pp. 11–18.

Booth, David. *Literacy Techniques: For Building Successful Readers and Writers*. York, M.E.: Stenhouse Publishers, 1996.

Bratcher, Suzanne. *Evaluating Children's Writing: A Handbook of Communication Choices for Classroom Teachers*. New York: St. Martin's Press, 1994.

Brown, Hazel, and Brian Cambourne. *Read and Retell: A Strategy for Whole Language / Natural Learning in the Classroom*. Westport, Conn.: Heinemann, 1990.

Buss, Kathleen, and Lee Karnowski. *Reading and Writing Literary Genres*. Newark, Del.: International Reading Association, 2000.

Calkins, L. M. *The Art of Teaching Writing*. Rev. ed. Portsmouth, N.H.: Heinemann, 1994.

Carstenn, Todd. "Metaphor Madness." *Writing Teacher* (May 1992): pp. 40–42.

Chilak, Judy. *"Success Is in the Details: Publishing to Validate Elementary Authors."* Language Arts, Vol. 76, No. 6 (July 1999): pp. 491–498.

Christelow, Eileen. *What Do Authors Do?* New York: Clarion, 1995.

Clark, Roy Peter. *Free to Write: A Journalist Teaches Young Writers.* Westport, Conn.: Heinemann, 1995.

Clemmons, Joan, and Lois Laase. *Language Arts Mini-Lessons: Step-by-Step Skill-Builders in Your Classroom.* New York: Scholastic, 1998. (Has sections on developing story ideas, understanding and using point of view, and writing dialogue.)

Cornett, Claudia E. "Beyond Retelling the Plot: Student-Led Discussions." *The Reading Teacher*, Vol. 50, No. 6 (March 1997): pp. 527–28.

Cramer, Ronald L. *Creative Power: The Nature and Nurture of Children's Writing.* Needham Heights, Mass.: Allyn & Bacon, 2001.

Danielson, Kathy Everts. *Integrating Reading and Writing through Children's Literature.* Needham Heights, Mass.: Allyn & Bacon, 1994.

Day, Frances Ann. *Latina and Latino Voices in Literature for Children and Teenagers.* Portsmouth, N.H.: Heinemann, 1997.

———. *Multicultural Voices in Contemporary Literature: A Resource for Teachers.* Westport, Conn.: Heinemann, 1999.

Denman, G. A. *Sit Tight, and I'll Swing You a Tail: Using and Writing Stories with Young People.* Portsmouth, N.H.: Heinemann, 1991.

Dionesio, Marie. "Responding to Literary Elements through Mini-lessons and Dialogue Journals." *English Journal,* Vol. 80, No. 1 (1991): pp. 40–44.

Ellis, Sarah. *The Young Writer's Companion.* Toronto, Ont.: Groundwood Books, 1999.

———. *From Reader to Writer: Teaching Writing through Classic Children's Books.* Toronto, Ont.: Groundwood Books, 2000.

Ernst, Karen. *Picturing Learning: Artists and Writers in the Classroom.* Westport, Conn.: Heinemann, 1994.

Fearn, Leif, and Nancy Farnan. *Writing Effectively: Helping Students Master the Conventions of Writing.* Needham Heights, Mass.: Allyn & Bacon, 1997. (Focuses on grammatical usage and how to teach conventions in a balanced writing program.)

Fiderer, A. *Teaching Writing: A Workshop Approach.* New York: Scholastic, 1998a.

———. *25 Mini-Lessons for Teaching Writing.* New York: Scholastic, 1998b.

Fletcher, Ralph. *What a Writer Needs.* Westport, Conn.: Heinemann, 1993.

Gallo, Donald R. *Authors' Insights: Turning Teenagers into Readers and Writers.* Portsmouth, N.H.: Boyton/Cook Publishers, 1992.

Gee, R. W. "Reading/Writing Workshops for the ESL Classroom." *TESOL Journal*, Vol. 5, No. 3 (1996): pp. 4–6.

Grant, Janet. *The Writing Coach: Strategies for Helping Students Develop Their Own Writing Voice.* York, M.E.: Stenhouse Publishers, 1992.

Graves, Donald. *Experiment with Fiction.* Westport, Conn.: Heinemann, 1989.

——. *A Fresh Look at Writing.* Portsmouth, N.H.: Heinemann, 1994.

Green, Judy. *The Ultimate Guide to Classroom Publishing.* York, M.E.: Stenhouse Publishers, 1999.

Greenlaw, James C. *English Language Arts and Reading on the Internet: A Resource for K–12 Teachers.* Upper Saddle River, N.J.: Prentice Hall, 2001. (Includes Web sites and links for children's and young adult literature authors and illustrators.)

Hansen, Jane. *When Writers Read.* Portsmouth, N.H.: Heinemann, 1987.

Hart-Hewins, Linda, and Jan Wells. *Better Books! Better Readers!: How to Choose, Use and Level Books for Children in Primary Grades.* York, M.E.: Stenhouse Publishers, 1999.

Harwayne, Shelley. *Lasting Impressions: Weaving Literature into the Writing Workshop.* Westport, Conn.: Heinemann, 1992.

Heine, Pat, et al. "Talking about Books: Strong Female Characters in Recent Children's Literature." *Language Arts*, Vol. 76, No. 5 (May 1999).

Hicks, Deborah. *"Narrative Discourse as Inner and Outer World."* Language Arts, Vol. 75, No. 1. (1998): pp. 28–34.

Hoyt-Goldsmith, Diane. *Pueblo Storyteller.* New York: Holiday House, 1992.

Jenkins, Carol Brennan. *Inside the Writing Portfolio: What We Need to Know to Assess Children's Writing.* Westport, Conn.: Heinemann, 1996.

——. *The Allure of Authors: Author Studies in the Elementary Classroom.* Westport, Conn.: Heinemann, 1999.

Lane, Barry. *After THE END: Teaching and Learning Creative Revision.* Westport, Conn.: Heinemann, 1993.

Lauritzen, Carol, and Michael Jaeger. *Integrating Learning through Story: The Narrative Curriculum.* Albany, N.Y.: Delmar, 1997.

Linse, Caroline T. *The Treasured Mailbox: How to Use Authentic Correspondence with Children, K–6.* Portsmouth, N.H.: Heinemann, 1997.

Lunsford, Susan H. "And They Wrote Happily Ever After." *Language Arts*, Vol. 74, No. 1 (January 1997): pp. 42–48.

Madigan, Dan and Victoria T. Koivu-Rybicki. *The Writing Lives of Children.* York, M.E.: Stenhouse Publishers, 1997.

Martinez, Miriam, and Marcia F. Nash. *"Bookalogues: Talking about Children's Literature: What a Character!"* Language Arts, Vol. 71, No. 5 (September 1994): pp. 368–374.

——. *Bookalogues:* Talking about Children's Books: Books for Literary Study." *Language Arts*, Vol. 74, No. 3 (March 1997): pp. 218–224.

Matz, Karl A. "Reading Children's Fiction: Finding the Author in the Work." *Writing Teacher* (January 1991): pp. 11–15.

McCarthy, Tara. *Teaching Literary Elements: Easy Strategies and Activities to Help Kids Explore and Enrich Their Experiences with Literature: Grades 4–8*. New York: Scholastic, 1997.

Mciver, Monette Coleman, and Shelby Anne Wolf. "The Power of the Conference Is the Power of Suggestion." *Language Arts*, Vol. 77, No. 1 (September 1999): pp. 5–61.

Mitchell, Diana. "Bringing Literary Terms to Life" *English Journal*, Vol. 84, No. 4 (April 1995): pp. 64–68.

Murray, Donald M. *Crafting a Life in Essay, Story, Poem*. Westport, Conn.: Heinemann, 1996.

Norton, Donna E. "Engaging Children in Literature: Modeling Inferencing and Characterization." *The Reading Teacher,* Vol. 46, No. 1 (September 1992): pp. 64–67.

——. "Engaging Children in Literature: Understanding Plot Structures." *The Reading Teacher*, Vol. 46, No. 3 (November 1992): pp. 254–258.

Otten, Charlotte F., and Gary D. Schmidt, eds. *The Voice of the Narrator in Children's Literature: Insights from Writers and Critics*. New York: Greenwood Press, 1989.

Ozvold, Lori. "Helping Students Add Voice to Their Writing." *Teaching-and-Change*, No. 4 (Summer 1997): pp. 312–324.

Palmer, Barbara C., Mary L. Hafner, and Marilyn Sharp. *Developing Cultural Literacy through the Writing Process: Empowering All Learners*. Needham Heights, Mass.: Allyn & Bacon, 1994.

Peregoy, Suzanne. *Reading, Writing & Learning in ESL: A Resource Book for K–12 Teachers*. Third Edition. Boston: Allyn & Bacon, 2001.

Peterson, R., and M. Eeds. *Grand Conversations: Literature Groups in Action*. New York: Scholastic, 1990.

Phinney, Margaret Yatsevitch. "Children 'Writing Themselves': A Glimpse at the Underbelly." *Language Arts*, Vol. 75, No. 1 (January 1998): pp. 19–27.

Robb, Laura. *Easy-to-Manage Reading & Writing Conferences: Practical Ideas for Making Conferences Work*. New York: Scholastic Trade, 1999.

Roberts, Patricia L. *Taking Humor Seriously in Children's Literature*. Lanham, Md.: Scarecrow Press, 1997.

Roe, Betty D., Suellen Alfred, and Sandy Smith. *Teaching through Stories: Yours, Mine, and Theirs*. Norwood, Mass.: Christopher-Gordon Publishers, 1998.

Routman, Regie. *Conversations: Strategies for Teaching, Learning, and Evaluating.* Westport, Conn.: Heinemann, 1999.

Saloff, Jamie L. *The Publishing Center: How to Create a Successful Publishing Center in Your School, Church, or Community Group.* Westport, Conn.: Heinemann, 1996.

Short, Kathy G., and Jerome C. Harste, with Carolyn Burke. *Creating Classrooms for Authors and Inquirers.* Westport, Conn.: Heinemann, 1996.

Simmons, Ray. "What Writers Know with Time." *Language Arts*, Vol. 73, No. 8 (December 1996): pp. 602–605.

Solley, Bobbie A. *Writers' Workshop: Reflections of Elementary and Middle School Teachers.* Needham Heights, Mass.: Allyn and Bacon, 2000.

Sudol, David, and Peg Sudol. "Putting Graves, Calkins, and Atwell into Practice and Perspective." *Language Arts*, Vol. 68, No. 4 (April 1991): pp. 292–300.

Takenishi, Michelle, and Hal Takenishi. Writing Pictures K–12: A Bridge to Writing Workshops. Norwood, Mass.: Christopher-Gordon, 1999.

Thomason, Tommy. *Writer to Writer: How to Conference Young Writers.* Norwood, Mass.: Christopher-Gordon, 1999.

Tucker, B. "Minds of Their Own: Visualizers Compose." *English Journal* (1995): pp. 27–31.

Tully, Marianne. *Helping Students Revise Their Writing.* New York: Scholastic, 1998. (Focuses on grades 2 and up.)

Vilscek, Elaine. *"Sensing Story Elements and Structure in Good Literature: The Models for Children's Writing."* Paper presented at the Annual Southwest Regional Conference of Authorship, Albuquerque, New Mexico, February 8–10, 1990.

Warner, Mary L. *Winning Ways of Coaching Writing.* Boston: Allyn & Bacon, 2001.

Weiss, Jaqueline Shachter. *Profiles in Children's Literature: Discussions with Authors, Artists, and Editors.* Lanham, Md.: Scarecrow Press, 2001.

Whitin, Phyllis. *Sketching Stories, Stretching Minds.* Portsmouth, N.H.: Heinemann, 1996.

Zancanella, Don. "On the Nature of Fiction Writing." *Language Arts*, Vol. 65, No. 3 (March 1988): pp. 238–244.

Ziegler, Alan. *The Writing Workshop: How to Teach Creative Writing.* Vol. 1. New York: Teachers and Writers Collaborative, 1981.

———. *The Writing Workshop: How to Teach Creative Writing.* Vol. 2. New York: Teachers and Writers Collaborative, 1984.

MULTICULTURAL LITERATURE

Anderson, Vickie. *Native Americans in Fiction: Guide to 765 Books for Librarians and Teachers, K–9*. Jefferson, N.C.: McFarland & Co. Pub., 1994.

Freeman, Evelyn, and Barbara Lehman. *Global Perspectives in Children's Literature*. Needham Heights, Mass.: Allyn & Bacon, 2001.

Hayes, Dwayne. *Something about the Author*. Farmington Hills, Mich.: The Gale Group, 2001. http://www.galegroup.com.

The Horn Book Guide, Interactive. Westport, Conn.: Heinemann, 1998. (A CD-ROM that reviews more than 29,000 children's and young adult books.)

Khorana, Meena. *Africa in Literature for Children and Young Adults: An Annotated Bibliography of English-Language Books*. Westport, Conn.: Greenwood Press, 1994.

Kruse, Ginny Moore, Kathleen T. Horning, and Megan Schliesman. *Multicultural Literature for Children and Young Adults: A Selected Listing of Books by and about People of Color. Volume 2: 1991–1996*. Madison: Regents of the University of Wisconsin System, 1997.

Miller-Lachman, L. *Our Friends, Our World: An Annotated Guide to Significant Multicultural Books for Children and Teenagers*. New Providence, N.J.: R. R. Bowker, 1992.

Multicultural Review. Newest books, videos, and software in the field of multicultural education. Published by Greenwood Publishing Group, Inc. http://www.mcreview.com.

Schon, Isabel. *The Best of Latino Heritage: A Guide to the Best Juvenile Books about Latino People and Cultures*. Lanham, Md.: Scarecrow Press, 1996.

Tomlinson, Carl. *Children's Books from Other Countries*. Lanham, Md.: Scarecrow Press, 1998.

Wood, Irene. *Culturally Diverse Videos, Audios, and CD-ROMs for Children and Young Adults*. New York: Neal-Schuman Publishers, 1999.

ASSESSMENT FROM CHAPTER 9

Atwell, Nancy. "Valuing and Evaluating," in *In the Middle: New Understandings about Writing, Reading, and Learning*. Portsmouth, N.H.: Heinemann, 1998.

Beaver, Teri. *The Author's Profile: Assessing Writing in Context*. York, M.E.: Stenhouse Publishers, 1998.

Bromley, Karen. "Attitudes about Writing: A K–3 Inventory." *Writing Teacher* (November 1991): pp. 9–11.

Fisher, Christie. "When Can We Write Another Book?" *Writing Teacher* (September 1993): pp. 28–30.

Runge, Pat. "Publishing: An Incentive to Revise." *Writing Teacher* (November 1994): pp. 21–22.

Spandel, Vicki. *Creating Writers through Six-Trait Writing Assessment and Instruction*. Reading, Mass.: Longman, 2000.

Index

About the Author

Norma Sadler is a professor at Boise State University in Idaho, where she teaches courses in children's literature, young adult literature, and creative writing. She has also led poetry workshops in both monolingual and bilingual classrooms. Dr. Sadler has presented at conferences on topics such as essay writing, creative writing, the use of multicultural read-aloud programs in classrooms, and research for professional development models in education. She has written articles, poetry, plays, and short stories for children, young adults, and adults.